To, Andrew

God Bless you Always

Felix Millan

M000218198

TOUGH GUY
GENTLE HEART

Felix Millán

with
Jane Allen Quevedo

INFINITY
PUBLISHING

All rights reserved. No part of this book shall be reproduced or transmitted in any form or by any means, electronic, mechanical, magnetic, photographic including photocopying, recording or by any information storage and retrieval system, without prior written permission of the publisher. No patent liability is assumed with respect to the use of the information contained herein. Although every precaution has been taken in the preparation of this book, the publisher and author assume no responsibility for errors or omissions. Neither is any liability assumed for damages resulting from the use of the information contained herein.

Copyright © 2012 by Felix Millán and Jane Allen Quevedo

Photo Credits: Front Cover, Associated Press. Back Cover, Ron Quick. All others by Jane Allen Quevedo unless otherwise attributed.

Player and Game Stats: The information used here was obtained free of charge from and is copyrighted by Retrosheet. Interested parties may contact Retosheet at "*www.retrosheet.org*".

ISBN 978-0-7414-7578-7 Paperback
ISBN 978-0-7414-7579-4 eBook
Library of Congress Control Number: 2012940701

Printed in the United States of America

Published August 2012 (With Revisions May 2013)

INFINITY PUBLISHING
1094 New DeHaven Street, Suite 100
West Conshohocken, PA 19428-2713
Toll-free (877) BUY BOOK
Local Phone (610) 941-9999
Fax (610) 941-9959
Info@buybooksontheweb.com
www.buybooksontheweb.com

Dedicated to

Mercy
My wife of fifty years

Bernie and Femerlie
My son and daughter

Mercedita and Vilmarie
Children of my heart

Our grandchildren
Jernie Rebeka
Victor
Elismarie
Maureen
Femerlix Alexandra
J-Lex

"And what does the Lord require of you

But to do justly,

To love mercy,

And to walk humbly with your God?"

Micah 6:8

Holy Bible. The New King James Version

Contents

Preface

BASEBALL FANS COULD BET their box of Cracker Jack that second baseman Felix Millán would get a hit when he stepped up to bat in the 1960s and 1970s. In his twelve-year career with the Atlanta Braves and New York Mets, he struck out fewer than 250 times in almost 5,800 plate appearances. For four years he held the National League's record for toughest guy to strike out. And as of 2012 he continues to hold the Braves' record for fewest strikeouts in a single season.

Another thing fans remember about Felix is the funny way he held his bat. He choked up so high it looked like he'd punch himself in the stomach when he swung at a pitch. This did not produce many home runs, but it helped make him a consistent second hitter to move runners on the bases ahead of him. Felix gave his teammates reason to place their confidence in him through his dependable hitting, quick action at second base, and unswerving dedication to the game he loved. The Puerto Rican made a big difference wherever he played, whether it was on the streets of his Caribbean homeland or in the Mets' run for the 1973 World Series.

Today, thirty-five years after his final major league game in 1977, some analysts consider Felix the best second baseman to ever play for the Braves and among the best with the Mets. (See References.) At the same time fans remember him as a humble and likeable player who stayed around after ball games signing autographs until the last kid had left the park.

I liked Felix immediately when a mutual friend introduced us in 2010. Although I found him a bit shy at first, he seemed genuinely warm and soon began sharing stories of his baseball days. Offered the opportunity to help write his story, I thought it would be fun. Certainly it would be like no other project I'd ever undertaken. And for a couple of important reasons, it would be one of the most challenging, too.

Even though Felix speaks English, I knew there would be times when he could best express himself in his own language. Unfortunately, my Spanish is limited, as is my knowledge of baseball. So, what made me think I could tackle a book about a major league baseball player from Puerto Rico? That's where my husband comes in.

Carlos is Puerto Rican and a baseball fan from way back. He was twelve years old when Hiram Bithorn went to the Cubs in 1942, the first player from the island to break into the major leagues. He also remembers the following year when Luis Olmo put on a Brooklyn Dodgers uniform for the first time. For many years Carlos was a loyal Dodgers fan.

Some time ago he took me to San Juan's Escambron where we stood outside the Parque Sixto Escobar, peering through a hole in the fence like a couple of kids waiting for a foul ball to come our way. This was Carlos' favorite place during winter baseball season when he was a boy. For a dollar he could catch a bus from his home in St. Just, arrive at the ballpark in San Juan in time for the morning game, catch a bus to Santurce for lunch with his grandmother, take a bus back to the ballpark for the afternoon game, and have enough change left over for return fare to St. Just at the end of the day.

Carlos' love of the sport only increased over the years. I brag that he is a walking baseball encyclopedia. He's the fan. I'm the storyteller. But could we work on a book together? I knew for sure I could not do it without him.

When we sat down for our first interview with Felix and his wife Mercy, I watched and listened as Carlos and Felix recalled how things used to be in Puerto Rico. Even though there's more than a decade's difference in their ages, they shared similar experiences of growing up on the island as well as their love of baseball. While I would eventually need to write about baseball, I was initially drawn to the events and circumstances that had shaped Felix's young life. Gradually those stories began to unfold, sometimes related in English and sometimes in Spanish.

He talked about the shyness that plagued his early childhood, his hardworking parents and their dreams for their children, the teachers who cut him some slack, and the "angels" who guided him along the way. There was a love story, too, as well as a spiritual journey. What I found, of course, were baseball stories woven throughout every other story: his first glove, the Gold Medal® uniform, his path to the major leagues, the people who helped him get there, the challenges and achievements he met as well as some lessons he learned along the way.

In early 2011 Carlos and I traveled to Yabucoa in the southeast corner of Puerto Rico to see where Felix grew up in the 1940s and 1950s. He took us to his childhood homes, schools and the ball field where he played as a teenager. We stopped by the mill where his father worked in the days when sugar was king in Puerto Rico, and the bakery where he bought a treat for his children on paydays. We visited the new baseball stadium in Yabucoa, too. There we surprised the mayor and some of his staff who were making plans for an upcoming event—the official naming ceremonies for the Felix Millán Stadium.

Putting Felix's stories together was even more fun than I had expected. I watched a lot of baseball games, read books I would not otherwise have read and searched the Internet for websites I did not know existed. I've been exposed to vocabulary, music, events, names, places, culture and history that not only expanded my knowledge, but enriched my life and I dare say, changed it.

It is not all here, of course. Time plays tricks with one's memory. Some interesting details are probably missing or related slightly different from how they actually occurred. Also, Felix hates to read. He wanted a short book. While the highlights of his career are here, I make no apologies for the shortage of statistics, analyses and detailed accounts of games. Those are easily available elsewhere.

My intent is to give readers some of the stories that don't show up in baseball stats or old newspaper clippings. Of course, these pages had to be about baseball, too. That was his passion and his career. But clearly there is a lot more to Felix Millán than double plays, base hits and batting averages. This is a book about a time and a place and the people who helped shape the character of a shy little kid who dared to dream big and grew up to see his dreams come true.

Jane Allen Quevedo

Introduction

I KNEW SOMETHING WAS WRONG in the autumn of 2011 when my husband did not have the energy to get out of bed before ten-thirty or eleven o'clock in the morning. We had recently returned from a month in Italy where Felix had worked for Major League Baseball. He had felt fine while we were away. But after only a few weeks at home, all he wanted to do was sleep late and sit around the house. This was not like Felix.

As long as I've known him, he has taken good care of himself. He exercises, has no weight problem, eats a healthy diet and does not abuse his body with alcohol, tobacco or drugs. When I suggested that he see a doctor, he thought I was overreacting. However, I knew from personal experience that his sudden episodes of lethargy and sleeping late were nothing to ignore. I pestered him until he finally agreed to see his doctor.

A routine physical examination revealed no problem. Thankfully, however, his doctor suggested further testing to make sure he had not missed anything serious. To shorten the story, within a few days Felix was admitted to the Cardiovascular Center of Puerto Rico and the Caribbean in San Juan in the care of Dr. José Rodriguez-Vega—the same cardiologist who had performed open-heart surgery on me in 2008. In our wildest dreams, we never expected to return to the hospital like this.

Even though the doctor said Felix appeared to be the picture of health, he ordered several tests to rule out any unseen problems. After five days of testing he had all the information he needed to give us a report and confront us with a serious decision. Indeed, there was a blockage, which sooner or later would require surgery. Felix looked at me as if to ask what he should do.

"Mercy cannot make this decision for you, Felix," the doctor told him. "It must be your decision."

Naturally, while Felix underwent all those tests, we had stayed in touch with our children every day. They were concerned. The girls, Femerlie and Mercedita, who live in Puerto Rico, hovered over us like a couple of mother hens. And we talked by phone at least once a day with our son Bernie in Florida.

When my husband decided not to delay surgery, Femerlie and Mercedita phoned everybody they knew in Florida and Puerto Rico, asking for prayers for their daddy as well as for the surgeon. I don't know how many people were praying for Felix, but we were grateful for each one.

Bernie was ready to catch the next flight to San Juan but I told him no. I remembered how Felix had dealt with my surgery and I knew our son would be the same way. Like his daddy, Bernie is physically strong. But he is so tenderhearted and emotional I knew he'd melt into a puddle of tears during those anxious hours that lay ahead of me. I already had enough on my mind without the added stress Bernie was sure to bring. I hoped he would understand.

Before the surgery, Felix and I had some time alone and we prayed together as we had so many times in our marriage. We struggled to be brave for each other, but of course, we were scared. After all, it was open-heart surgery and we knew the risks. Felix put himself in God's care and we asked for the hands of heaven to guide Dr. Rodriguez-Vega throughout the delicate procedure.

Behind my smiles and kisses my heart was heavy as I watched my husband wheeled away on a gurney toward the operating room. Knowing the surgery could be a matter of several hours, I prepared myself for a long wait. My girls did their best to be strong for me, reminding me over and over that hundreds of friends and family were praying for us.

Felix and I had been through a lot in the fifty years we had known each other. He was a lonely soldier boy with big ideas when we met, and I did my best to help him realize his dreams. I don't know how many times I pitched practice balls for him to bat, or cheered from the stands when he made an incredible double play. Nor did I keep track of all the hours of waiting while he signed autographs for fans. We had prayed for children, for dying parents, for difficult decisions, for healing, for faith. I had every reason to believe God would see us through this crisis, too.

However, I did not expect Dr. Rodriguez-Vega to walk into the waiting room only ninety minutes after Felix went to surgery.

"What's wrong?" I asked.

"Everything is fine, Mercy. It's all over and it went very well," he said, giving me a hug for encouragement.

"Thank God," I sighed in relief.

"I've done about five thousand open-heart surgeries, Mercy, but I've never had one go as smoothly as this one," he told me.

"Oh, I can tell you why," I said without pause.

Perhaps the doctor was expecting me to praise his surgical skills because when I said it was Jesus, he gave me a patronizing look as if to say, "Oh, yeah?"

"I tell you, Doctor, people all over Puerto Rico and Florida have been praying for you," I continued. "I know Jesus was guiding your hands and that is why it went smoothly."

Seeing he could never convince me otherwise, he finally admitted that I might possibly be right.

In the following pages, my husband shares stories of his life and career. It has been a blessed life and I've been blessed to share it. Baseball fans will enjoy reliving some of the highlights of his days with the Atlanta Braves and New York Mets. Beyond baseball, readers will learn where he came from, the values he developed from the time he was a young boy, and some of the challenges he faced as well as lessons he learned along the way. I'm delighted to introduce you to my guy. This is the Felix Millán you've never met until now.

Mercy Millán

1

Papi's Dreams

I COULD HARDLY WAIT for school to let out. Stuffing my tablet into my desk, I slid my butt across the smooth wooden bench beneath me until I could stretch one foot into the narrow aisle next to my seat. On the other side of the classroom I saw Lon and Ernesto preparing for our great escape, too. But I could run faster than either of them. I'd be the first one out the door and first to catch a glimpse of Officer Huertas' Jeep coming up the road.

The Yabucoa police department sponsored our league and Officer Huertas had the job of driving us boys to practice and games. About ten of us would crowd inside his Jeep, which looked like something left over from World War II. Because few families in the Yabucoa Valley owned cars in the 1950s, riding around in that Jeep was almost as much fun for a team of eight- and nine-year-old boys as playing baseball.

Suddenly I noticed the classroom had turned silent. Briefly taking my eyes away from the doorway, I turned to the front of the room and directly into the gaze of Señorita Quiñones. I could see she was prepared to hold the entire class hostage until she had my undivided attention. Moving back toward the center of my seat I gave her a timid smile, revealing the small gap where my front teeth failed to meet. While I never saw her lips move even the slightest, I'm sure she smiled back at me. After only a moment that seemed more like several minutes, she finally pronounced those magic words, "Class dismissed." It was time to play ball!

Of course, I had played ball in my barrio or neighborhood ever since I could whittle a bat from the branch of a guava tree. I knew how to make a firm albeit lopsided ball by winding string and tape around a smaller ball, perhaps one "borrowed" from some girl's set of jacks. When I could get a piece of heavy canvas—the kind used to cover truckloads of sugarcane—I could make a decent glove by stuffing it with newspaper. But on the league, the policemen saw that we boys had real gloves and bats and balls.

Three of my brothers and I were especially good ballplayers, which pleased nobody more than our Papi (Pahpee). Like a lot of fathers in Puerto Rico, Victor Millán dreamed of a son growing up to become a professional baseball player. As a boy he had been a good player himself, a catcher. While he may have briefly entertained the idea of a baseball career, standing little more than five feet tall, he was too short to take it seriously. Besides, as soon as he began working in the sugar mill and making a little money any such dreams quickly vanished.

When Papi married Anastasia Martinez, they immediately started a family. There had been eleven babies in all, but one died at birth and another died at a very young age. The remaining nine of us looked like stair steps when we stood next to each other: Victor, Ramonita, me (the one they called Nacho), Mercedes, Cecilio, Jesusa, Silverio, Domingo and Heriberto.

Any of Papi's dreams for himself gradually became his dreams for us. Above all he insisted that we finish school. He had not. A hot-tempered unruly child, he hated school and did not take to discipline to the point of instigating fist fights with his teacher. After attending first grade for three years, he gave up. My grandparents kept him home and as a result he never learned to read or write. My mother, affectionately called Mami (Mah-mee), took care of any tasks in our home that required reading or writing.

Papi walked about five miles to and from work at the Central Roig sugar processing plant in the southeast corner of the island where we lived. The mill offered steady work for only six months a year. At thirty-five cents an hour he earned barely enough to support our family above the starvation level. It was a hot dirty place to work, especially when time came to burn the bagasse. That is the tough fiber left after the sweet juice is extracted from the cane. Papi tended a huge furnace called *la caldera* in which the bagasse was burned.

Fridays were special whenever I had a ball game, but doubly so during sugarcane harvest because that was payday at the mill. With a little money in his pocket, Papi always stopped at the Panadería Ortiz, a bakery where for ten cents he could buy a special treat for us children. As soon as I finished playing ball, I ran all the way home to get there before Papi came from work. I'd wait in front of our house, watching for him to turn the corner and head toward home. His hair would be covered with large flakes of ash, his skin shiny with sweat and his face so black with soot he was barely recognizable. And in his hand he carried our treat, a long slender loaf of pan or bread, its golden crust still warm from the oven. Mami tore it apart in equal portions, making sure we each received our share.

One of my favorite childhood memories is of Papi playing the guiro, a percussion instrument he carved from a hollow gourd. He'd find some music to his liking on the radio, preferably Puerto Rican folksongs that tell stories about the island and its people. He scraped the guiro with a stick to which he had attached a row of thin wire tines. This created a dry rasping sound and added counterpoint to the Latin tunes. Papi was very good on the guiro. In fact, he once competed for best player in Puerto Rico. My brother Cecilio had a knack for playing the guiro, too. Sometimes we kids would dance when Papi played. Our little brown bodies would twist and spin like toy trompos or tops while keeping time to the Latin rhythms.

We were as poor as any family reliant on sugarcane for a livelihood in Puerto Rico in the 1940s and 1950s. But we were a big happy family—all living together under the roof of a little house that had no electricity. It was the only life I knew. I guess that's why I was surprised the day Papi sent me to Juan Martin to live with my grandparents. I was ten years old. He said I was big enough to help with chores and I'd be good company for the older couple. It also meant I had to walk almost an hour to and from school every day.

"What about baseball, Papi?" I asked.

"Don't worry, Nacho," he said. "You can play at school."

El Cerro del Calvario. My early childhood home is at the right, now overgrown with weeds and in disrepair. As a young boy this is where I watched for Papi to return from work. On pay-days he always brought home a ten-cent loaf of freshly baked bread for me and my brothers and sisters to share.

Yabucoa about 1950. This is how it looked when I was a boy growing up here. Photographer: David Groh, from the Lehman Collection, courtesy of the Luis Muñoz Marin Foundation.

I remember when sugarcane blanketed the Yabucoa Valley. During the burn-off prior to harvest these fields were ablaze and the air thick with smoke. Large flakes of ash fell from the sky like black snow. (Photo by Jack Delano, 1941, Library of Congress Prints and Photographs Division)

2

Bare Feet and Baseball

MY GRANDPARENTS HAD A FLOCK of chickens I had
to take care of. Also, Papi's brother, my Tío (uncle) Pedro,
kept five fighting cocks in cages at their place. I had to water
and feed them, too. He gave me strict orders to make sure
those roosters did not get out and fight each other. And he
came around once a week to make sure I did a good job. One
time when I wasn't looking, two of the roosters somehow
managed to get into a fight through the bars of their cages
and one damaged his spurs. Tío Pedro was so mad he gave
me a whipping I never forgot. Years later I learned those
roosters belonged to someone else who paid my uncle to
keep them. Of course, I never saw any of the money.

I lived in Juan Martin with my grandparents off and on
throughout my school days. While my grandfather was an
easy going guy, my grandmother was serious. I don't remember ever seeing her smile. As a young boy, of course, I

could not imagine what hardships she might have endured raising a large family in Puerto Rico in the 1920s and 1930s.

I knew I was special to my grandparents and I liked living with them. At times, however, I was lonely staying in the country with the elderly couple. After all, I was accustomed to being around a lot of brothers and sisters and a neighborhood full of boys ready to pick up a ball game at a moment's notice.

At the same time, in the country I enjoyed the luxury of my own room. My grandparents' house was a simple five-room wood structure with a corrugated zinc roof. I liked that roof especially during rainy season. I'd lie on my bed listening to the rain pound like thousands of little hammers over my head. At my parents' home I would have had to share not only a room with my brothers, but a bed, too.

The Yabucoa Valley was like the Garden of Eden to me. Surrounded by a green ring of mountains, the valley stretched out over hundreds of acres blanketed with long-leafed sugarcane plants. Those fields seemed to ebb and flow like the waves of the nearby Caribbean Sea when a warm breeze moved across the valley, sometimes making it difficult to tell exactly where the fields ended and the sea began.

This was my home far away from a larger world I knew only from picture books, newspapers, radio and a young boy's imagination. When I wasn't feeding chickens or doing other errands for my grandparents, I likely could be found fishing in a nearby stream or climbing a mango tree for some of the sweet fruit that grew in abundance around there.

After a while I befriended a neighbor named Paulino Ortiz. I called him Don Paulino, using the common Spanish title of courtesy. He was one of the people I refer to as an angel in my life. He took me under his wing, paid special notice of me and in many ways took good care of me. Every kid needs someone like that.

Don Paulino grew a lot of fruit and vegetables on his farm and I used to take them to market for him. He let me take his horse. Rising long before daybreak, I'd drape two large baskets across the animal's back. After filling them with avocadoes, mangoes, papayas and any other produce that was ready, I'd mount the horse and ride to Yabucoa. I liked the rhythmic sound of the animal's hoofs clipping against the pavement in the quiet of the predawn hours. I must have looked something like el jibarito, the fellow in the Rafael Hernandez composition, "Lamento Borincano" ("Lament of the Puerto Rican").

Unlike the poor country man in the song, however, I always managed to sell Don Paulino's fruits and vegetables. He trusted me to deliver his products, get the right price and return with his money. As a result he always treated me right. When I came back from the city, he'd give me five dollars and tell me to buy some food.

I never missed an opportunity to make a little spending money when I was a kid. I even collected bags of grass called coitre, which I sold to people who raised rabbits. They paid me twenty-five cents for about a bushel of grass.

At my grandparents' home I missed baseball more than anything else. There was no one to play with and little time to play—except at school, which was in Yabucoa. Juan Martin is on Highway 901, the main road connecting Yabucoa and the ocean. To reach the city I had to walk past fields of sugarcane that reached twice my height on both sides of the road. There wasn't much traffic on the long ribbon of gray asphalt that lay between me and school every morning. Other than an occasional truck or a team of oxen hauling a wagon, I saw little more than some fire-colored flamboyan trees and a few country houses scattered amongst the sugarcane.

An hour's walk every morning and afternoon gave me plenty of time alone in my own thoughts. I usually daydreamed about baseball, imagining myself all grown up and playing in the big leagues. In truth, I didn't mind those long walks. What bothered me was that I had no shoes. I was the only barefoot kid in fifth grade. My feet were always dirty and the soles were tough as leather.

While it was fairly common in Puerto Rico for first and second graders to go to school barefoot, by the time we were in fifth grade most of us had shoes. The government occasionally distributed free shoes and I'd wear mine until there was nothing left to them but a sour smell. In fact, I had one pair that stunk so bad Papi dug a hole and buried them behind our house.

To make matters worse for me, in fifth grade I was smitten with a little dark-haired girl named Dominga. I would sit quietly at my desk while keeping an eye on her in hopes she'd glance my way. At the same time I struggled to hide my feet by placing them as far under my seat as they would reach. I lived in constant fear of our teacher calling me to the front of the classroom where Dominga and everybody else could see my dirty bare feet.

Papi and Mami eventually moved to a house about five minutes from the Juan B. Huyke School in Juan Martin where I attended seventh through ninth grades. I'd sometimes sneak over there from school on the pretense of going to the bathroom. I'd ask my teacher for permission to leave the classroom, run home, drink a cup of good Puerto Rican coffee, and be back at my desk in the same time it would have taken me to go to the bathroom. Somehow I never got caught. I don't know whether the teacher simply overlooked my absence or could not imagine that I'd do anything other than what I told her.

My reputation as a trustworthy kid made me something of a teachers' pet. In fact, one of my high school teachers, Professor Guadalupe Rivera, used to give me five dollars and excuse me from class every day to buy his lunch. I'd walk downtown and for about three dollars I could get a mound of white rice smothered in pinto beans with some meatballs or chicken on the side. In addition to giving me a much-appreciated break from the classroom, Professor Rivera always let me keep the change.

I may have been the kind of kid a teacher or neighbor could depend on, but I was extremely shy around my classmates. In fact, in kindergarten I would not even stay to eat and play with them at lunchtime. Instead, I'd run all the way home looking forward to a plate of Mami's warm rice and beans. Often, however, I found nothing to eat.

Mami went out every day to scour the countryside for whatever wild fruit and vegetables she could gather for free. When Papi was working, he'd buy rice and beans by the hundred-pound bag for about four-and-one-half cents a pound. Sometimes, provided he was working, he could buy on credit, too. But when he wasn't working nobody would give him credit. When the mill closed for the season, our family income amounted to what he made at odd jobs and whatever money Mami earned from doing laundry for people in the city.

On days when I found no food at home, I'd cry all the way back to school, promising myself when I grew up I would have a big refrigerator filled with food. I'd make sure Papi and Mami had plenty to eat, too. I remember asking God to give me a chance to be somebody when I grew up so I could help my parents.

We were not a particularly religious family. Like most Puerto Ricans, we were Catholic. Papi went to church occasionally, but as I recall Mami and we kids went only on special occasions such as Easter and Christmas. When I think about it, she probably could not muster up the energy to get nine kids ready for church on Sunday mornings. Besides, there was so much work to be done around our house—meals to cook, laundry to wash, kids demanding her attention. There was no end to it.

Even though she knew how to delegate chores and assign the older children to care for the younger ones, Mami was busy all day long. Her hands moved from task to task as fast as a New York traffic cop in rush hour. Feeding our large family was a huge job. I remember going with her to the countryside to dig wild sweet potatoes. She sent me to climb a tree to pick some ripe breadfruit, a starchy rough-skinned tropical fruit about the size of a very large grapefruit. Mami knew when the different fruits and vegetables were ready for harvest and exactly where to find them.

She also took in washing and ironings—on top of doing our own family's large laundry. Sometimes I'd go to the river with her on washday. She'd scrub the clothes by hand and then spread them over large rocks to dry in the sun. The following day she had a huge stack of clothes to starch and iron. With the temperature outdoors soaring around ninety degrees, Mami was inside our house pressing clothes with an iron heated by hot coals. I used to fan or blow on the coals to keep the iron hot for her. After pressing clothes all day, she avoided going outdoors in the cool night air for fear of catching a cold or worse, pneumonia. That was a common belief among many on the island in those days.

The next morning Mami walked to Yabucoa to deliver the freshly starched and pressed laundries and collect her earnings. I can still see her hiding a little bit of money by tying it in a knot in the corner of a handkerchief. She had a tough life, and while I never heard her complain, I rarely saw her smile either.

Before moving to Juan Martin, my parents had lived in a little house in the barrio called El Cerro del Calvario, which means The Hill of Calvary. According to legend a man was hanged in this barrio sometime between 1518 and 1873 when slavery was practiced in Puerto Rico. I always felt there was something special about my community. From the religious reference in the name of our barrio to the landmark church on the plaza, in Yabucoa there were always reminders of man's connection to God, none more clearly than the angels depicted on the city's coat of arms. These two figures represent the heavenly companions that accompany one in the journey of life. While I was blessed by some earthly angels, I believe heavenly angels guided me throughout my life, too.

I learned at a very young age that God is in control of things in this world, but I could pray for what I needed. One of my earliest childhood prayers was answered when I discovered my school served free lunches. My older brother Victor learned of it first. When I saw him eating at school, I figured I could swallow my shyness long enough to fill my empty stomach.

Even though I soon grew taller than my older brother, I always looked up to him and wanted to do whatever he did. When Victor played baseball, I wanted to play, too. The truth is, all the boys in our neighborhood played baseball and I would have played even if he had not.

I was in junior high school when a woman living near my grandparents made my first baseball uniform. Several of my teammates and I hired her to make them from some cotton flour sacks. I think she did not know English because she carefully positioned the colorful Gold Medal® logo right across the seats of our pants. While it had nothing to do with corporate sponsorship, in those days Gold Medal® sure got a lot of free advertising from little kids wearing homemade uniforms of discarded flour sacks.

The woman charged us each thirty-five cents. My problem was I had only twenty-one cents. She finally let me have a uniform even though I could make only a "down payment." I reasoned that I had brought her a lot of business by recommending her to my teammates. I went back several years later to pay my fourteen-cent debt, but by that time she had moved away.

As a kid I was a Yankees fan. I'd listen to Buck Canel on the radio giving play-by-play accounts in Spanish of their home games. To enhance his broadcast he used sound effects such as a loud whack when a batter hit the ball. Sometimes he even added howling wind in the background, giving me the idea that Americans played baseball in snowstorms. I didn't think I would like to play in cold weather.

I had two baseball heroes. One was Jaime Almendro, shortstop for San Juan. But my biggest hero was undoubtedly the legendary Lou Gehrig, who died in 1941. While I never saw Gehrig play ball or even heard one of his games on radio, I idolized the guy. Growing up in a culture where stories of baseball heroes passed from generation to generation like old folktales, I was especially drawn to the larger-than-life stories of the king of grand slams who played more than two thousand consecutive ball games.

I could not imagine anything better in life than to play more than two thousand ball games like Lou Gehrig had. That was my boyhood dream. I knew at an early age I wanted to grow up to be just like him. I wanted to live like him, play like him and I once declared I even wanted to die like him. Of course, I changed my young mind about that last part a long time ago.

The one place I was never shy was the ball field. I had a natural talent for the game and learned quickly. As my game improved, my confidence slowly grew and while I never fully overcame it, my severe shyness slowly began to fade. Before long I learned that whistling was a good way to distract an opposing team's batters. I perfected a distinctive, annoying and persistent whistle that I used to my full advantage.

Baseball eventually made me one of the most popular kids at school. Everybody wanted Nacho on their team. My Tía (aunt) Frances was responsible for calling me Nacho when I was just a little guy. She mistakenly thought it was the nickname for Bernardo, my middle name. By the time she learned it was actually the nickname for Ignacio, which means fire, I was answering to Nacho. Apparently the name suited me because to this day I'm known as Nacho in Yabucoa.

As a kid I played baseball every chance I had—recess, after school, on weekends. Of course, I had to work baseball around my chores—or to be more truthful, work my chores around baseball. Even though I lived with my grandparents, Papi was my boss and I had to answer to him if my chores were not done. Fortunately, he loved baseball. That made it pretty easy to rearrange my chores to accommodate my games. In fact, Papi was my biggest fan, never missing a game or practice and bragging to anybody within hearing range, "That's my son."

By the time I was fourteen or fifteen years old, I played on a Class C team in Yabucoa. The manager, Maneco Rodriguez, was the first of many good teachers I would have over the years. During the week we'd play at the high school, sometimes getting out of classes early for a ball game. On weekends we traveled by bus to compete with other teams in our region of the island. It seemed like everybody in Yabucoa was a baseball fan. They'd fill the benches of the old stadium where we used to play our home games. Of course, Papi was right there cheering for me.

Until high school I did not own a baseball glove. I either borrowed one or used one supplied by my team or league. I remember the day Ivan "Ivy" Ortiz, brother of the owner of the bakery where Papi used to buy bread on paydays, took me to the original Mudafort Sport Center in Santurce. He let me choose any glove in the store.

I played shortstop at that time and I wanted a glove that allowed me to catch the ball with an open hand and get rid of it quickly. I knew exactly what I needed and I tried on gloves until I found a soft pliable Rawlings mitt of good leather that fit my hand perfectly. I was really proud of that glove. I had it for a long time.

Most of the time I preferred playing baseball over going to school, perhaps with the exception of home economics class. In those days, all students—guys and girls—had to learn to cook, wash dishes, set a table and even to sew. In fact, my first assignment was to make an apron. For me, the best thing about the class was my teacher, Señorita Berrios. She was so young and pretty that I wanted to fail the course just so I could spend another year with her.

Thankfully, I was a good student as well as a good ballplayer because my heart was not in school. Not only was my mind somewhere on a baseball field, reading always put me to sleep. No matter the subject, whenever I'd start reading, I'd doze off. To this day, I hate to read. I had one teacher who either finally gave up on me or, as I'd like to believe, understood my situation. After playing ball late on Sunday nights, like clockwork, I would fall asleep the next day in Matilda Matthews' tenth-grade English class. My classmates did all sorts of things to keep me awake. They even tried singing loudly until Mrs. Matthews stopped them.

"Let him sleep," she'd say. "He played ball last night."

How many kids have a teacher like that? I don't know, but could it be that she excused me for sleeping in class because she could see a future for me beyond the Yabucoa Valley? That was certainly my father's dream.

I remember when my brothers and I went to work in the sugarcane fields. We were teenagers and wanted to make a little spending money. Of course, Papi found out and immediately ordered us to quit, fearful that we would not finish school if we started making money. As far as he was concerned, education came first. He was the boss and he gave us no choice. As it turned out, every one of Victor Millán's children graduated from high school and none of us ever worked in the sugarcane fields or the sugar mill.

After my older brother and sister finished school, they went to work near San Juan and began helping our parents with household expenses. Victor worked in construction with Tío Andres, our father's brother, while Ramonita did housework for a family in Río Piedras. I was in high school at that time, making a name for myself as a star baseball player and entertaining my dream of becoming a major league baseball player.

My whole family had big hopes for me and supported my dream. Victor always made sure I had the clothes and equipment I needed, especially my uniforms and shoes. He was a good ballplayer himself. However, he was too short to consider a professional baseball career. My youngest brothers, Domingo and Heriberto, turned out to be good players, too. Both would eventually play amateur baseball in Puerto Rico.

I graduated from high school with no money for college and no plans for the future. Most of my friends were in the same position. One day they came up with the idea of joining the U.S. Army and for lack of a better plan, I went along with them.

I was scared the day I found Papi at the top of the chimney of the Central Roig sugar mill. It had closed for the season and he was hired to paint the tall structure that even today remains a landmark in the Yabucoa Valley.

3

For the Love of Mercy

WHAT WAS I DOING in the Army? I hated getting up at
three a.m., crawling on my belly like a snake under a blanket
of barbed wires, loaded down with a heavy pack on my back
and dodging blank bullets in the dark. Not only did I dislike
the training, I could not understand what anybody said.
Away from Puerto Rico for the first time in my life, the only
words I remembered from Mrs. Matthews' English class
were "mother," "father" and "thank you." There's not much
call for those words in the Army.

If struggling with English commands was not tough
enough, I was assigned to the Signal Corps and had to learn
Morse code. I was terrible at it. One series of beep-beep-
beeps didn't sound any different to me than another. On top
of that, I don't particularly like heights and the Army wanted
to make a lineman of me. I watched some of the other soldiers scale up and down telephone poles with nothing more

than little pegs for support. Then I saw one of the guys fall several feet to the ground.

"What have I gotten myself into?" I thought.

Of all my friends who took the Army test, only two of us passed. Hector Trinta would make a career of the Army. Not me. Almost before I knew it, I had boarded a plane headed to boot camp in South Carolina. I was homesick before we ever left the airport and would have given anything to go right back home. But I had joined the Army voluntarily. There would be no going home for two long years.

I found the Army especially tough in large part because of the language. Even though I occasionally ran into other Spanish-speaking soldiers on base, I never felt so alone in all my life—hundreds of miles away from my family and a world apart from my island home in the Caribbean. Sure, I wasn't the first nor would I be the last lonely soldier in the Army. That offered little comfort when it was happening to me.

I was jealous of the soldiers who received mail from home. They'd get letters from their girlfriends. They had places to go on weekends. I stayed in the barracks alone wishing I had somewhere to go and somebody to go with me. I thought it would be nice to have a girlfriend, a Spanish-speaking girlfriend. But all I had to look forward to was another week of trying to follow orders I could not understand and dreading my turn to climb the telephone pole.

I had not been in the Army very long before I began thinking about the life I wanted someday. I dreamed of getting married and having a family. I'd grown up in a happy family and wanted the same for myself. I prayed that when the time came, God would bring the right woman into my life. Meanwhile, I had to deal with the Army.

I wandered over to the USO one day after I had transferred to Fort Gordon near Augusta, Georgia, and was surprised to find a baseball game in progress. I had no idea the Army played baseball. After watching the game, I went to the manager, a Lieutenant Smith, and with the little English I knew, I asked if I could try out for the team.

"Sure," he said. "Come to practice next Thursday and show me what you can do."

"Just wait 'til you see what I can do," I thought to myself.

I was one of the first players to show up at the ball field the following week. I felt like I had found a little bit of home. After practice I went back to my barracks hoping I had made a favorable impression even though the lieutenant never let on whether I had or not. A day or two went by before I received the order to pack up my equipment and report to the Special Services barracks. I had made the team.

Suddenly Army life was not so bad after all because the Army treats its athletes very well. There were road trips in summer to play ball at the other bases, and we could go to the mess hall at any time for something to eat. Coming from a home where the food supply was often scarce, that was a big deal for me.

I started out playing shortstop until I hurt my arm. After that I played first base. I spent most of my Army days playing baseball, returning to my original barracks only during the off-season.

While other soldiers looked forward to mail call, of course, I didn't. That's why I was really surprised the day a letter arrived addressed to me. My brother's girlfriend sent a photograph of a girl she knew and suggested that I write to her. Not only was the girl in the picture pretty. She had a nice name. Mercy.

Not wasting any time, I immediately composed a letter, dropped it in the mail and waited for a reply. I expected to soon begin receiving letters like the other soldiers. I waited and waited and waited, but mail call brought no letter for me. After a few days, I thought perhaps my letter had been lost in the mail, so I wrote another one. A few more days went by and still no reply. I thought maybe this girl is playing hard to get. I needed to let her know I don't give up easily. So I wrote another letter.

Finally, my wait ended. I was the happiest soldier on base the day I received my first letter from Mercy. Soon our letters were flying back and forth between Georgia and Puerto Rico three or four times a week. This went on for almost two years. After a while I wondered if I was falling in love. Or, were Mercy's letters just helping me through those awful lonesome days in the Army?

We began anticipating my discharge coming up in July 1962 and made plans to meet as soon as I returned to Puerto Rico. Again I wasted no time. Instead of going to Yabucoa, I went directly to Tío Andres' home near Río Piedras because I wanted to be near Mercy.

It was wonderful to be in Puerto Rico again surrounded with all the familiar sights, smells and sounds of home. I didn't have to translate every word spoken to me or worry that I'd give an inappropriate response because I didn't fully understand a question or comment.

Of course, the main thing on my mind was meeting Mercy. I went to her house the very next day. I was so nervous I could literally feel my heart pounding in my chest. I hoped she would like me. Was this really the girl I loved? Or was I just a lonesome soldier who had fallen in love with the dream of love?

When Mercy came to the door and I set eyes on her for the first time all of my words seemed stuck in my throat. She could not have weighed even a hundred pounds.

"She's so skinny," I thought.

Then she smiled at me and I smiled back. That's all it took. I was definitely in love. Mercy was even prettier in person than in her pictures. After only one meeting I knew she was the girl I wanted to marry.

For the next six months I lived with my Tío Andres and Tía Oti, who treated me like one of their own kids. I enjoyed being with them, of course, but mostly I enjoyed being close enough to my girlfriend that I could see her every evening.

It didn't take long for me to learn that Mercy was a praying girl. All the while I had been in the Army praying to meet the girl of my dreams, she had been praying for a husband. We did not realize it at the time, but I know we were praying for each other. I think God had His hand over us from the very beginning—long before my brother's girlfriend slipped Mercy's picture into an envelope and dropped it in the mail.

Mercy's father, however, had some serious questions about me. He was very protective of his little girl. All he knew about me was that I was fresh out of the Army and taking up a lot of his daughter's time. Without our knowledge, he set out on a personal investigation to check out whether I qualified as a proper suitor.

Since he did not drive or own a car, he hired someone to take him to Yabucoa. Right away he learned that almost everyone in town knew Nacho Millán, the young baseball player with the quick glove and annoying whistle. People assured him I was a good kid, not a troublemaker, and most important, I was not married and never had been married. Those were the main things he wanted to hear.

I happened to be in Yabucoa that day but totally unaware of his visit. Needless to say, I was surprised when he discovered me on a street corner playing cards with some of my friends. I think it was good that he had already heard favorable reports about me. Otherwise, he might not have stayed around long enough to learn I was a good guy for his daughter.

Even though I passed his test with high honors and he gave Mercy the all clear to continue seeing me, he never allowed me to take her on a date. Our entire courtship occurred on his front porch. Traditionally, Puerto Rican young women did not go out alone with young men. While this custom was beginning to change by the early 1960s, Mercy's father was from the old school. He would let me know when I could visit her and how long I could stay.

He had a particularly unusual way of letting me know when my visit was over. With a toothbrush in hand he stood near a window where he knew I was sure to see him. Then he began to brush his teeth. This ritual was my signal to leave. In time I won him over, and even though he never allowed me to take her on a date, he said yes when I asked if he'd allow me to marry his daughter.

I think Mercy was already secretly making wedding plans when I proposed. Or you might say when I gave her an ultimatum.

"If we don't get married by the end of the year, I'm going back to Yabucoa," I said.

I don't know why I put it that way. I loved her. Of course, I would have waited if she was not ready to get married. Fortunately, she was ready.

With every visit I became more certain that Mercy was the right girl for me. For one thing, she seemed genuinely interested in my love of baseball. I knew I needed a wife who shared my passion for the game.

I also noticed the way she cared for a little neighbor girl named Mercedita. Mercy had been the child's babysitter from the time she was born. I could see that she would be a great mother. This was very important to me because I wanted a big family. However, before we could get married and start having babies, I needed a job. After all, I had to assure Mercy's father that I could provide for his daughter.

I got in touch with Antonio Medina, owner of the Yabucoa Double-A amateur baseball team. He remembered me from my ball-playing days in high school and gave me a job on his team for about seventy-five dollars a week. Of course, that was just a step toward my dream of one day playing professional baseball.

Scouts from the major leagues regularly came around the Caribbean looking for prospective players. For most of us young guys in the 1960s, a career in the major leagues would remain only a dream no matter how much we wanted it or how hard we worked for it. Only about a dozen Puerto Ricans played in the major leagues at that time. In the twenty years following Hiram Bithorn's break into the big leagues in 1942, fewer than two dozen Puerto Ricans had fulfilled that dream, several for no more than a season or less. I watched with interest as that number slowly grew.

I was just a kid dazzling hometown fans in Yabucoa when a guy from Carolina named Roberto Clemente began his legendary career with the Pittsburgh Pirates. About the same time the St. Louis Cardinals signed Luis Arroyo and the next year Felix Mantilla went to the Milwaukee Braves. More names from my island continued showing up on the player rosters of major league teams—Orlando Cepeda and José Pagan went to the San Francisco Giants, Juan Pizarro to the Braves and Julio Gotay to the Cardinals, to name a few.

With every Puerto Rican who broke into the big leagues in the 1950s and early 1960s my hopes increased. Things were beginning to change for ballplayers of Puerto Rico. Yet

I could not imagine a time when Latinos would make up a third of the major league players as they do today. One hard lesson I had learned in the Army remained true in 1962. Baseball in the United States was a white man's game—an English-speaking white man's game. But I did not let that discourage me. I embraced my dream of playing major league baseball like I embraced the young woman who would share it with me.

And so it was that Mercy and I began our lives together on seventy-five dollars a week and a big dream. We were married December 21, 1962, at Cristo Rey Catholic Church in Río Piedras with about a hundred friends and family members present. We had six attendants, including little Mercedita who carried our rings. Mercy's father escorted his daughter down the aisle. He also had the good sense to pitch a tent in his yard in case of inclement weather for the reception. That was good planning because it rained like crazy.

People said the rain was a good sign—like showers of blessings—and we would need a big caldero or cauldron to contain all our happiness. In our case, it was true. Marrying Mercy was the best decision I made in my life. From the day we were married she helped put my dreams in order. Her aunt rented us a little house for twenty-five dollars a month. The small cottage was perfect for two young kids madly in love.

I did well on the Yabucoa team. Before long I was getting a lot of attention as one of its best players. When the Ponce team prepared for a series in Colombia in 1963, they asked me to join them as a reinforcement player. Scouts from the States were coming in and out all the time watching us practice and I did my best to impress them.

One of the scouts was a guy named Felix Delgado. I remember the day he drew me aside and asked the question I'd waited to hear ever since I was a barefoot kid taking care of roosters in Juan Martin.

"Felix, how would you like to play professional baseball?" he said.

He didn't have to ask twice. My prayers were answered. I had the wife of my dreams and Delgado was offering me the career opportunity of a lifetime. After only a year and a half with the Yabucoa team, I signed a contract with the Kansas City Athletics (A's) as an amateur free agent. I was on my way to Daytona Beach, Florida, to join their Class A farm team. While this was an important step, I knew I had a long way to go to realize my ultimate dream. The question remained: Would I be the next Puerto Rican and the first guy from Yabucoa to play major league baseball?

4

Minor Details

I SHOWED UP IN DAYTONA BEACH ready to play ball, planning to give it everything I had—train hard, learn quickly and move right on to the big leagues in Kansas City. But it didn't work out exactly the way I planned. First of all, Delgado changed my position. I had signed with the A's as a first baseman. However, after watching me for a while, he believed I would be much better on second base.

I had a good hand and I could move quickly to make double plays. Delgado saw when the ball hit my glove I got rid of it quickly. I was a hustler. I could dive for the ball, stretch, get up and get rid of it without even thinking. Being fast on my feet was critical in order to avoid injury by a runner sliding into second base. I agreed that with the right training, second base would be a good fit for me. It meant I had to concentrate on throwing harder, jumping higher, running faster and turning double plays.

Not everything I had to learn was on the ball field. There was the matter of my English or the lack of it, and a culture far different from what I was used to in Puerto Rico. Even though my Caribbean island home was a territory of the United States, its language and cultural roots lay in more than four hundred years of Spanish rule following its discovery by Christopher Columbus in 1493. To put it in perspective, Puerto Rico had been a United States territory only sixty-six years when I arrived at Daytona Beach in 1964. I may have been a United States citizen, but everything about me was Puertorriqueño. I spoke Spanish. I ate Puerto Rican food. I danced to Latin music. I celebrated Spanish holidays. I was one hundred percent Puerto Rican.

I arrived in the States during a turbulent time. The country continued to grieve the assassination of President John Kennedy a few months earlier. Tensions with Cuba, Panama and other Latin American countries were high, and the United States was divided over the Vietnam War. While President Lyndon Johnson signed the Civil Rights Act in July, racial discontent continued. This was a strange world for me.

Baseball clubs were beginning to be more open to blacks and Latinos by 1964 than they had been in the '40s and '50s, but certain areas of the country were not. I had never experienced racial prejudice in Puerto Rico. There I could go into any restaurant and stay in any hotel I could afford. That was not the case in the States, especially in the South.

When I traveled with the Daytona team, the white players always stayed in nice hotels while we Latinos and blacks were put up in second-class places away from the rest of the team. When we stopped to eat, we stayed in the bus while the white players went inside the restaurant. I remember a fair-skinned Cuban on our team who was permitted to eat with the white players. He brought food to the bus for us. I hated the way we were treated and I looked forward to playing in the big leagues. Certainly, I would not face prejudice there.

Racial issues aside, and even though I enjoyed playing baseball in the States, I was happy when the season ended and it was time to go home. I hoped to play winter ball in Puerto Rico to keep up my game and continue developing my second-base skills, not to mention that I needed a paycheck.

Delgado and I went to see Hiram Quevas in San Juan, hoping to find a spot for me on an amateur team. I waited outside Quevas' office while the two men talked. I don't know whether they left the door open intentionally, but I could hear every word they said. My heart dropped when I heard Quevas say he had nothing for me. Fortunately, Delgado had a backup plan.

"How would you like to play in Venezuela, Felix?" he said.

I didn't care where I played as long as I played. At least in Venezuela I could speak Spanish and I would not need someone to bring my meals to me in a bus.

What I remember most about that winter in Venezuela had nothing to do with my baseball skills. First of all, someone stole my Rawlings glove, the one from Mudafort's. I'd worn that glove until the inside was as smooth as the skin of a ripe mango and I was sick about losing it. The other problem had to do with political unrest and an unsuccessful takeover attempt of the Venezuelan government. Our league finally dissolved and I went back home where the A's had negotiated an exclusive contract for me to play with the Caguas Criollos (Creoles) in the Puerto Rican Professional Baseball League.

After a year at Daytona Beach, time came for the A's to sign me to the majors. Otherwise, another team could pick me up, which is exactly what happened. While I had done well in Daytona, the A's did not sign me and the Atlanta Braves came along and got me for only twenty-five hundred dollars. That was one of my first lessons in the business of major league baseball.

Instead of going to Kansas City in 1965, Mercy and I moved across the United States to Yakima, Washington, where I joined the Braves A team in the Northwest League. For a guy who grew up on a tropical island, I did not know what climate to expect in the Northwest. I remembered the sound effects of wind howling in the background of Buck Canel's radio broadcasts. Although it did not snow while I was in Yakima, the weather turned off unseasonably cold in the middle of July, confirming my childhood fear that I would not like playing ball in cold weather. However, Yakima turned out to be good for me in every other way. First of all, I did not have to deal with racism. My problem was finding someone in Yakima to cut my hair. I went to a white barber who looked at my Afro and shook his head.

"I don't know how to cut that," he said.

I did not take it personally. I thanked him politely, and asked one of my teammates to cut my hair.

The best thing that happened to me in Yakima had nothing to do with weather, race or a haircut. This is where I met Hub Kittle.

Hub was a legend in his own time—manager, trainer, pitching coach, bus driver. You name it, he did it. He was the best teacher a ballplayer could have and I was blessed to learn from him. Hub knew I had what it took to get to the majors. He saw my potential as a solid second hitter to move runners on the bases ahead of me.

"Hit the ball and run, Felix. You're good at it," he said.

The best thing Hub ever did for me came when I was in a slump, hitting in the low .200s. Knowing he had to do something, he drew me aside.

"Felix, at three o'clock tomorrow we're going to the ballpark," he said. "Let's try to meet the ball."

He worked with me every day, studying me like a book and suggesting ways to improve my swing. He had me crouch down a bit and elevate my left elbow about even with my cheekbone. When he told me to choke up on the bat, I began to see a difference right away. I varied the choke until I found the best position for the most control of the bat. In fact, I choked up about six inches. It looked like I would poke the bat into my belly when I swung it. But it worked. Pretty soon I was hitting the ball wherever it was pitched. In no time I was hitting .326.

I thought if this weird batting stance takes my hitting from .200 to well over .300, I'd better stick with it. Choking up gave me the control I needed to get line drives anywhere on the field. But it did not produce home runs, which is why batters no longer do it. Today's game is all about power. I was one of the last players to choke the bat like that.

As far as my bat was concerned, I found a 36-ounce or 33-ounce one worked best for me, depending on the weather. I liked the lighter one in July and August when the temperature was hot.

When the Braves moved from Yakima to the Texas League, I went to Austin. I loved playing for Hub. However, I was not planning on a career in the minors. After about three years I grew impatient to get to the big leagues. I was batting .308 to .311, making double plays and proving that I was one tough guy to strike out. Clearly, I had accomplished everything my coaches had asked of me. I could jump. I could throw. I could jump and throw at the same time. I could scoop a grounder faster than you can say Yabucoa, and I had avoided injury. My fielding average in the minors was a decent .958.

I do not know how many times I heard a coach predict that if I had a good spring, I'd be going to the majors. Then it would not happen. I remember the spring I hit about .385. I knew for sure I was headed to the big leagues, but no. I was told I needed more experience in the minors. I needed more play time. I needed to develop my skills. I needed more work on double plays. I needed to work on this or that. I knew I was as quick as any second baseman in the majors. I was a good hitter and a good fielder. I could play with the best of them. After a while I became discouraged.

There was more at stake than just fulfilling a boyhood dream of playing major league baseball. I was having a tough time financially. I had a wife and we wanted to start a family, but we were hardly making ends meet on a minor league salary of about eight hundred dollars a month. I was ready to call it quits.

"It's no use staying here," I told Mercy. "Let's go home."

"You don't want to have regrets later," she warned me. "Give it another chance."

Not long after that, Hub called me to his room one night following a game in El Paso. It was a short meeting because he had only one question on his mind.

"Felix, do you think you can hit the big league pitchers?" he asked.

He knew the answer before I could get the words out of my mouth.

"Of course, I can!"

"Well, get ready," he said. "You're leaving for Atlanta tomorrow."

Thank God I had listened to Mercy.

5

Brave Beginnings

I'LL NEVER FORGET MY FIRST DAY with the Atlanta
Braves. I don't think it was just a coincidence that Hank
Aaron drew me aside.

"Where are you staying tonight?" he asked.

When I told him I'd get a hotel room, he insisted that I
go home with him. The next morning he wanted to know
how I planned to get around town.

"I'll take a bus," I said.

He held out his hand and offered me a set of car keys.

"Take my Camaro," he said.

He not only let me use his car. He also requested that I
room with him when we were on the road. We would room
together all the time I played with the Braves.

Aaron had a practice of taking under his wing some of
the young black and Latino players. Actually, I was his
second Puerto Rican roommate named Felix because he had

roomed with Felix Mantilla, about ten years my senior, when the Braves were in Milwaukee.

I admired Aaron—as a human being as well as a ballplayer. He was a good guy both in and out of the game, and he treated me right. The most important advice he ever gave me was to be grateful for the opportunity to play major league baseball. He didn't like to party and neither did I. When we were on the road, we often passed the time in our hotel room playing cards while the other guys were out on the town.

Alcohol was never a problem for me. I give Papi a lot of credit for being a good role model in that regard because other than occasionally smoking a cigar, he never used alcohol or tobacco. I had no interest in drinking or partying. I just wanted to play baseball.

I joined the Braves in Atlanta in their first season after moving from Milwaukee. This was the team of Aaron, Eddie Mathews, Joe Torre, Felipe Alou and Phil Niekro. I was proud to be part of their club. Wearing the Atlanta Braves' uniform No. 11, I made my major league debut June 2, 1966, in a game against the San Francisco Giants.

I found it a bit intimidating the first time I stepped into the batter's box before a crowd of nearly 30,000 fans. However, those feelings all went away as soon as I got a base hit my first time at the plate. Unfortunately for us Braves, San Francisco took that game 5-0.

The Braves had paid me twenty-five hundred dollars to sign, and after ninety days in the majors, I expected a progression bonus. It was about five thousand dollars or so, and

Mercy and I were really counting on it. However, only three days short of my ninety days, Braves manager Billy Hitchcock asked to meet me for breakfast. I had a gut feeling it meant bad news. My fears were correct.

"Felix, we're sending you to Richmond," he said.

My heart sank. Nothing at that point in my career could make me feel worse than going back to the minors after finally making it to a major league team. I had paid my dues in the minors. I had accomplished everything asked of me and had not incurred a single injury. I knew I was good enough for the big leagues. I could not believe the words I heard coming from Hitchcock.

"We'd rather see you play every day in Triple-A than sit on the bench here doing nothing," he said.

This was not what I wanted to hear. Sure, I wanted to play every day, but not in the minors. I played a good game for the Braves when they played me. In my first three months, I played second base in only 25 games, achieving 54 putouts, 56 assists, and 12 double plays. I made only 3 errors and had a .973 fielding average. In 91 times at bat, I struck out only 6 times, and earned a .275 batting average. As far as I was concerned, the Braves didn't play me enough. The truth was they had a lot of money invested in their regular second baseman Woody Woodward.

Sitting across the breakfast table from Hitchcock, I kept my mouth shut, politely listening to all his reasons for sending me to Richmond. He said I needed to work on my double plays and concentrate on avoiding injury. Second base can be a dangerous spot because of potential collisions with runners sliding into base. I knew that. He did not say anything I did not already know. Of course, I would do what was necessary to protect myself on the field, but any baseball player knows injuries come with the game.

"You'll get some good experience in Richmond," he said.

If that was supposed to make me feel good, it did not. While his words went right over my head, I knew better than to argue the point. In those days a player did not protest or ask for a trade when the organization made a move he did not like. There were fewer teams than today and the competition was great. If I didn't agree to what was asked of me, I knew some other young guy was out there waiting on the sidelines to take my place. I had worked hard and waited a long time to get into the major leagues. I would not risk saying anything to jeopardize my future in baseball. I kept my thoughts to myself.

I remember a conversation with Wayne Minshew from *The Atlanta Constitution,* who later became the Braves' public relations director. He tried in vain to console me, saying that I didn't deserve to be sent back to the minors. He had seen these kinds of things happen to other players and he tried to convince me that it's the way the game is played in the major leagues.

"It's a business decision," he said.

"Don't worry," I snapped. "I'll be back soon." In truth, I made that promise more to myself than to Minshew.

I went to Richmond feeling more determined than ever to prove myself. Looking back, I realize that it really was a matter of business. And I have to admit it was a turning point in my career, beginning the day I met Luman "Lum" Harris, manager of the Triple-A Richmond Braves. He was undoubtedly one of the best teachers I had in my baseball career. Nobody ever believed in me like Lum. I worked hard to live up to his expectations.

In Richmond I teamed up with Bobby Cox, who retired as manager of the Braves in 2010. Together we created a lot of excitement for minor league baseball in our race to take the 1967 International League pennant. Dubbed the "gold dust twins" by sports writer Laurence Leonard, Cox and I drew huge crowds, pulling in as many as eighteen thousand fans to a three-game set with Rochester.

The bigger the crowds, the harder I played—and the more I whistled. I whistled when I was happy. I whistled under pressure. I whistled to distract opposing batters. Someone counted that I whistled three hundred and sixty-five times in one game alone.

All the energy and excitement going on in Virginia did not go unnoticed by Braves management in Atlanta. Paul Richards, vice president of operations, told Leonard he had not seen such big crowds attending minor league games in a long time.

With a batting average of .310, I was named minor league player of the year. I never knew what Hitchcock thought of my work in Richmond. It really did not matter anymore because his days with Atlanta were almost over. The Braves were getting a new manager.

I never made a habit of asking for personal favors, but I made two exceptions while I was in Richmond. The first was when my brother Silverio was killed. We were in Montreal when I received the news. As soon as Lum heard, he told me to catch a plane to Puerto Rico. I asked for a second favor when Mercy's mother was dying of cancer. With only one month remaining in the 1967 season, I asked Lum if I could leave early to join Mercy and spend some time with my mother-in-law. His response surprised me.

"Are you a doctor, Felix?" he asked.

I thought that was a strange question.

"Look, there's nothing you can do for her there," he continued. "And this is an important month for you here."

That's when he told me he was going to Atlanta as the new Braves manager and I was going with him to be his second baseman. Nothing could have made me happier. Lum had been rooting for me ever since the day I arrived in Richmond. I was excited about going to Atlanta with him. This was the best news he could give me, and I should not have given it a second thought. But the timing was all wrong. I needed to be with Mercy and her mother.

"You need to be in Atlanta," he said. "You'll get some big league experience in the final month of this season and you'll be ready to play for me next season. If you go to Puerto Rico now, you'll miss an important month that could help you."

I had no choice.

I am pictured here (second from right) with three important people in my baseball career. From left, Hank Aaron was my roommate all the years I played with the Braves; Luman Harris took me with him when he went to Atlanta after managing the Triple-A Richmond team; and teammate Clete Boyer later recommended me to the Yokohama Taiyo Whales. My life would have been another story were it not for these men. This photo was taken at spring training in West Palm Beach, Florida, March 1, 1969. (AP Photo/ Ray Howard)

6

Brave Years

AFTER A MONTH IN ATLANTA I went to Puerto Rico, arriving there the same day Mercy's mother died. I thank God I could be with her before she fell asleep for the last time.

I was back playing with the Criollos again that winter, all the while eagerly anticipating spring training with the Braves. I remember promising Papi when I got to Atlanta I would be the most "hustlingest" ballplayer in camp.

Some may have been surprised to see me going to the Braves as long as Woodward was still there, but Lum had a lot of confidence in me. He knew what I could do and I knew he would play me. It was no secret that he had a pretty high opinion of my abilities as a second baseman. In fact, later in my career he would call me the best second baseman in the National League, and "'the closest thing to a perfect ballplayer'" he had ever seen (Wayne Lockwood, *Baseball Digest*, October 1969). I worked hard to live up to Lum's expectations—showing up to play every day with a smile on my face. I managed to earn the confidence of the other players, too. In Lockwood's words, "Millán does his job with a quiet competence in all departments that inspires respect from both sides of the diamond."

One of the first things I did when I returned to Atlanta was choose another number. My No. 11 had gone to Deron Johnson, a good hitter traded in from the Cincinnati Reds. I chose 17 for no other reason than it looked almost like an 11. I was never superstitious about my uniform number.

Opening day in Atlanta, April 12, 1968, found me in the starting lineup with Hank Aaron, Felipe Alou, Clete Boyer, Sonny Jackson, Deron Johnson, Joe Torre, Mike Lum and Pat Jarvis. Cincinnati's Pete Rose hit the first ball of the game, which I picked up and threw to first base for the first out of my first game back with the Braves. We won 4-3.

Taking my place in the Braves lineup alongside some baseball superstars and legends I admired, I looked forward to a good season, maybe even a championship. Just as I had promised Papi, I hustled all the time. By mid-season I was getting a fair amount of attention in the press. *Sports Illustrated* writer Gary Ronberg called me a "sweet player" (July 22, 1968): "He can hit, he can hit and run, bunt for a hit, sacrifice and finagle a base on balls. He can run and slide and he can scramble back up and run some more."

Before long, my playing style earned me the nickname Kit or El Gatito in Spanish. Milo Hamilton, play-by-play announcer for the Braves, commented that I moved like a kitten. He shortened it to Kit and the name stuck. I later "grew up" to be called Cat. Whenever I went to bat in Atlanta, the ballpark organist played the theme song from the television program *Felix the Cat.*

Kitten, Kit or Cat. Any of those nicknames was easier for English speakers to pronounce than my last name. Millán is "mee-yahn" in Spanish. Some compared it to saying "me on second" or "filet mignon." It didn't matter to me how anybody pronounced my name as long as they called me to play ball.

The Braves had been stuck in the middle of the National League standings for several seasons and were long overdue for the top spot. I admit I had ambitions of helping them get there in 1968. We got off to a good start and were holding onto second place even with some injuries on the bench. Before long I had joined the injured list, too.

It was the eighth inning of a game with Cincinnati on June 19. A former Richmond teammate, Clay Carrol, was on the mound. I was going for my fifth hit when he nailed my hand. I missed more than two weeks of games and watched helplessly as my Braves slipped to third and then fourth place.

Coach Jim Busby told Ronberg, "Without Felix in there we just weren't the same club."

By the end of the season, the Braves had managed to win only half of our games, leaving us fifth in the league again.

I played 149 of 162 games in the regular 1968 season, behind Aaron's 151 and Alou's 158. I had made a total of 91 double plays, 438 assists and 330 putouts, earning a .980

fielding average. In 570 times at bat, I had 165 hits and struck out only 26 times.

The next year brought some big changes to major league baseball. For one, the American and National leagues were each divided into two six-team leagues. This required the addition of four new franchises. The American League added the Los Angeles Angels and Washington Senators while the National League added the Montreal Expos and San Diego Padres.

Further, each league was divided into East and West divisions. The Braves went to the National League West Division along with the San Francisco Giants, Cincinnati Reds, Los Angeles Dodgers, Houston Astros and San Diego Padres. The National League East Division included the New York Mets, Chicago Cubs, Pittsburgh Pirates, St. Louis Cardinals, Philadelphia Phillies and Montreal Expos. At the end of the regular baseball season, the top-ranking team in each division competed in a best-of-five championship series to determine the team to go to the World Series.

Two other changes came in 1969. The strike zone was reduced to the area over home plate between the batter's armpits and top of his knees. Also, the pitching mound was lowered five inches. Neither of these changes had much effect on my game. My batting story continued to be hit and run. Move the runners on base ahead of me. Because I was not a home run hitter, I must mention our game against San Francisco on April 8 in Atlanta.

I always stood close to the plate, and in the first inning of that game, Giants pitcher Gaylord Perry caught me on the cheek. My eye swelled up like I'd been on the receiving end of a prize fighter's glove. Lum wanted to take me out.

"Why didn't you take me out before he hit me?" I said, letting him know I planned to stay in the game.

I came right back in the second inning with a single. I flied out in the fourth and was up again in the sixth with the bases loaded. Bob Didier and Ralph Garr were on base when Perry intentionally walked Alou, not taking the risk of letting him hit a home run. He loaded the bases knowing I was the next batter up. Clearly, he did not expect any more from me than a ground ball. In other words, an easy out on any base. He already had made me look bad when he caught my cheek. Then, adding insult to injury, he walked Alou. I was furious.

I went to the plate, my cheek still swollen the size of a lemon. I assumed my usual stance, choking the bat and holding my left arm where I could see Perry directly over my elbow. I had to make sure he did not get that easy out he presumed he had. I usually allowed the first pitch to pass, but I don't think I did that day. All I remember is when the ball came fast and right over the plate where I needed it, I swung my choked-up bat with every ounce of power my 172-pound body could muster. I made amazing contact and before I realized what had happened, the ball was gone—left of center, over the fence and all the way out of the park. Home run!

The crowd went wild. Didier crossed home plate, followed by Garr, then Alou and finally me. I glanced up in the stands where Mercy sat. But she wasn't sitting. She was jumping up and down, waving her arms and cheering like crazy. I had hit a grand slam. If I ever felt the pure joy of playing baseball, it was at that moment.

Pumped with excitement, I raced into the dugout expecting my teammates to rally around me. Instead I faced a sea of solemnity. Nobody uttered a word. They acted as if I had done nothing. No smiles. No slaps on my back.

"What's wrong with you guys?" I wondered.

After all, the player who didn't hit home runs had just cleared the bases. About the time I began to settle down, they broke into cheers, whooping and hollering and making all kinds of commotion. I had been a victim of the silent treatment, an ages-old gesture of rookie acceptance in the major leagues. Never in my life have I been more happily ignored. They made me feel great.

That was my only grand slam in the United States. While home runs were not my job, I did manage to hit 22 of them in my major league career. I was the guy others depended on to get a hit. In 652 times at bat, I struck out only 35 times in 1969, a Braves' season record I continue to hold today. Also, I was the first Brave to play all 162 games of a regular season. That is a team record I held from 1969 to 1982 and now share with Dale Murphy, Andruw Jones and Jeff Francoeur.

As far as my career and stats were concerned, I proved to be one of the league's best defensive second basemen in 1969 with 373 putouts, 444 assists and a .980 fielding percentage. I had 174 hits with 23 doubles, 6 home runs, and 57 runs batted in, achieving a .267 batting average.

We finished the season with 93 wins. At last, the Braves had the top spot in the National League West. We were on our way to the first ever National League Championship Series and favored to take that title, too. However, the Mets of 1969 were on a roll.

The famous Miracle Mets story is one best known in baseball history. That team had never finished a season higher than ninth place since joining the National League in 1962. Winning only 18 of their first 41 games, 1969 looked like a repeat performance. Then things took a dramatic turn. They won 39 of their last 50 games, finishing with 100 wins and 62 losses, due in large part to the excellent pitching of Tom Seaver.

This was the team everyone expected the Braves to beat for the National League championship. I remember before the series began, someone asked manager Gil Hodges which of the Braves he expected to give them trouble. He said there were four, quickly naming the first three. Then he paused. He could not remember the fourth.

"That kid. I don't know his name," he said. "The one on second."

He was talking about me. It was not my style to draw attention to myself. I had a job to do and I knew my teammates depended on me. I concentrated on perfecting my game and doing my best. The smile on my face was evidence of how much I enjoyed my work.

We mistakenly thought we were ready for the Mets, but they swept us in three games. Then they went on to take the

1969 World Series title, defeating the American League's Baltimore Orioles in five games.

Despite our loss, 1969 was a great year for me personally. I received my first Gold Glove, made my first All-Star team and best of all, God blessed Mercy and me with our first child—a son. We named him Felix Bernardo and called him Bernie.

Even though the Braves dropped to fifth place in the National League West the following year, there were some notable celebrations, too. For one, 1970 marked the one hundredth anniversary of the franchise. Also, Aaron got his 3,000th hit, the ninth man in baseball history to do so.

My most memorable game of 1970 was on July 6 when I had the chance to get six hits in a nine-inning game. Until then only nineteen players in the National League had ever achieved six for six. No player in the Braves club had ever done it.

We were up against the Giants in Atlanta and I was doing what I was supposed to do, hit and run. I had a single in the first inning, triple in the third, singles in the fourth and fifth and a double in the seventh. At the end of the seventh inning, I had five hits in five times at bat. Lum thought I should take a breather, but I would not hear of it. My teammates were pulling for me.

"Anybody can go five for five," Bob Aspromonte said. "Not too many get six for six. You have the chance."

I knew I'd never forgive myself if I let the opportunity pass. Sure enough, I managed to pull off another single in the eighth inning, giving me six for six in a nine-inning game, a

Braves' record I held for 37 years until Willie Harris tied it in 2007. The Braves took that game 12-4.

While 1970 may not have been a good year for the Braves, it was a good one for me. I batted .310, my major league career high. I had 25 doubles, 100 runs and 16 steals, also career highs. I was selected to the All-Star team for the second time. In 142 games and 590 times at bat, I struck out only 23 times.

Throughout the following season the eyes of the baseball world were on Aaron and San Francisco's Willie Mays in their race to break Babe Ruth's record of 714 homers. Not only did I enjoy watching Aaron's home run numbers grow. I hit ahead of him, which meant if I was on base I scored when he got a home run.

A Braves game I'll never forget was against the New York Mets on August 5, 1971. I remember it for two reasons. First, the game went 17 innings. Second, I made 6 double plays. It was a night game in Atlanta that lasted nearly four and one-half hours. We scored a run in the third inning and the Mets tied it up in the fifth. Twelve innings later the Braves finally scored the winning run.

I liked playing the Mets, especially when I had a chance to go to New York City. I had a lot of friends there and could always count on getting together with the fans and other Latino players for some good Spanish cooking. It never mattered that I was playing against their hometown team. To the Puerto Ricans of New York I was Puertorriqueño and that's what mattered to them.

I made 120 double plays in 1971, my highest season for double plays. I was selected to the National League's All-Star team for the third year in a row. By the end of the season, the Braves had won slightly more than half of our games, putting us third in the league. I played 143 games that season. With only 22 strikeouts in 577 times at bat, I ranked for the first time as the toughest player to strike out in the National League.

The next year brought big changes. Eddie Mathews, Braves third baseman from 1952 to 1966, replaced Lum as manager in midseason. It was probably the right move for the club. Nevertheless, it was difficult for me personally to say goodbye to my friend Lum. I played only 125 games in 1972 due to an injured hamstring muscle. My batting average slipped to .257 while my fielding average improved to .987. I also received my second Gold Glove.

By the end of the season, it was clear the Braves needed better pitching. As one of their best infielders, I knew I was a good candidate for a trade. It came as no surprise when Mathews broke the news to me. He tried to be kind and kept apologizing because he knew I loved the Braves. I'd been with them a long time. It would take a while for me to adjust to another team, another city and new fans. Leaving the Braves at the end of 1972 also meant that I would not be with them the next season when everybody expected Aaron to break Ruth's record. I wished Mathews would skip the apologies and get to the point.

"I'm sorry, Felix, but you are going to the Mets," he finally said.

Did I hear correctly? The Mets? What was there to be sorry for? Had Mathews forgotten I'm Puertorriqueño? Did he have any idea how many Puerto Ricans lived in New York City? I was elated.

The only thing that could make me happier than going to the Mets was the birth of our second child, a beautiful little girl born shortly after I returned to Puerto Rico for the winter season.

When I left the Braves at the end of 1972, I had played in 799 major league regular season games. While that is the number in the record books, I had also played 404 minor league games plus all the winter league games in Puerto Rico. Somewhere along the way I lost exact count of all my games, but I never stopped being grateful for the opportunity to live the dream of a lifetime.

Back home in Puerto Rico I enjoyed another season of winter ball. Throughout my career I would play seventeen seasons with the Caguas Criollos. Part of that time I also worked as manager and general manager, and one winter I managed the Lobos de Arecibo (Arecibo Wolves). Of course, nobody enjoyed winter ball in Puerto Rico more than Papi.

7

Proud Latino

MY FATHER WANTED me and my brothers and sisters to get an education because it meant we would have a better life than he and Mami had been able to provide for us. He instilled in me a desire to succeed in whatever I did. From the time I was a little boy, I wanted to do well and give him and Mami some of the things they never had. Soon after I started making money in baseball I bought them a new house.

At that time they lived on top of a hill in La Pica where they had moved when I was in high school. With no road leading up there, a dangerously steep footpath offered the only access to their house. No ambulance or fire equipment could reach them in case of emergency. I worried about their safety and wellbeing. When Mercy and I discovered some houses under construction in Yabucoa, we decided to buy one for them. Knowing they would likely object if they learned of it beforehand, we made it a surprise.

As soon as construction was finished, Mercy went to work painting and furnishing all the rooms, complete with those luxuries Mami had never had such as a range, washing machine and refrigerator. As I expected, my parents were not exactly excited with our plan to move them into the city. But that all changed after they moved in and got used to the idea. I was happy Mami no longer had to cook over an open fire or scrub laundry by hand. And nothing gave me more pleasure than to stock her refrigerator with plenty of food.

My mother never watched me play baseball. She claimed she did not want to see me get hurt. Perhaps the truth was she did not think she could afford to sit around watching grown boys play games when she had so much work to do at home.

Papi on the other hand, never missed a game when I played in Puerto Rico. Although he did not drive a car, he always found someone eager to take him to a game in exchange for a free ticket. And even if he could not read, he managed to find my name and pictures in the sports pages of the newspaper. He always had a collection of clippings to show off to his friends.

Papi was a friendly guy. He loved to talk with people, especially when the topic of conversation turned to his son the major league baseball player. However, he had never seen me play a major league game in person. When I made an All-Star team, Mercy and I decided to bring him to Atlanta.

Because he was nervous about flying in an airplane, Mercy went to Puerto Rico and accompanied him on his flight. I looked forward to showing him around, introducing him to some of the players and giving him a good time while he was with us. But he never gave me the chance. He insisted on going back to Puerto Rico the very next day after arriving in Atlanta—without ever seeing a game. No matter how we tried to persuade him to stay for at least one game, he would not hear of it. He complained that people were not friendly.

"Nobody talks to me," he said.

Of course, the problem was he didn't speak English. Mercy was so angry she refused to fly back to San Juan with him and he had to go alone. I know he was scared. I think the real problem was he missed my mother.

Even though Papi had been a good ballplayer in his younger days, and even if given an opportunity to play in the major leagues, I believe it would have been extremely difficult for him to adjust to life in the United States. While baseball has been and continues to be a ticket out of poverty for a lot of Latinos, many are unable to deal with the challenges that come with it, such as separation from their homeland and family, not to mention the language barrier. In his day Papi would also have had to deal with the racial issues of the '40s and '50s. I'm glad he didn't have to go through that.

By the time I came to the United States in 1964, baseball was changing. Black players such as Jackie Robinson, Satchel Paige, Willie Mays and Hank Aaron had made the transition from the old Negro Leagues to the major leagues. Additionally, the Latino players before me had begun to pave the way for future players from the Caribbean. I'm indebted to Roberto Clemente, Felix Mantilla, Orlando Cepeda and the others who had to deal with prejudice because of their skin color and Latino roots. While laws and rules may have changed, it would take time to erase a long history of stigmas and practices, written or unwritten.

Language and pronunciation have been problematic for Latinos for as long as we have played major league sports in the United States. I hated it when writers imitated my Spanish-flavored broken English by spelling my comments phonetically. It was embarrassing and demeaning and made me look silly. If I did not understand a question or gave a misapplied response, I ended up the brunt of someone's joke. The word that gave me the most trouble was "very." Even when I intentionally enunciated the "v," I'd be quoted as having pronounced a "b." If I said, "Baseball has been very good to me," I was quoted in broken English, "Béisbol been bery good to me."

I wonder how those writers would have felt had the situation been reversed. After all, we Latinos did our best and worked hard to become bilingual. Fortunately, major league baseball clubs now have language schools which are a great help to their non-English speaking players. Unfortunately, though it may no longer be socially and politically correct, poking fun at the expense of Spanish-speaking athletes continues today.

Language was one thing. Color and culture were something else. While I may not have had it as bad as many players before me, I dealt with my share of discrimination in the

'60s and '70s. Some things I could change with practice, such as my English. What I could not change, of course, was being Latino. I remember one time when a pitcher gave me what was obviously a bad ball.

"St-r-r-r-ike!" the umpire bellowed.

"What do you mean?" I protested. "That was a bad ball."

I was totally unprepared for his sarcastic response: "But it's better than cutting sugarcane in Puerto Rico."

The words burned to my core. Why did he have to say that? That man had no idea of the pride I have in my Latino heritage. I will never forget nor regret where I came from no matter how humble it may have been. When I played baseball, I played for Puerto Rico. I knew I represented my island and I wanted my people to be proud of me.

Another experience I'll not forget was a trip I made from Florida to Texas with Glen Clark. We had been teammates since Yakima and both had gone to Austin with Kittle. After the Braves' spring training in West Palm Beach, time came for us to return to Austin. Clark had a beautiful Thunderbird and invited me to ride with him. Coming from Texas, maybe he was accustomed to the treatment we received in that part of the country. I was not. We stopped for lunch at a restaurant in Mississippi. This guy met us at the front door and pointed toward the back of the building.

"If you boys want something to eat, go 'round to the kitchen," he said.

Clark and I looked at each other. Obviously, he'd dealt with this kind of situation before.

"No way," I said. "You can stay if you want to but I'm not eating here."

We got back into his beautiful Thunderbird and drove down the road until we found a 7-Eleven®. For the rest of the trip 7-Eleven® was our restaurant.

Our managers and coaches always encouraged us to mix it up and sit together when we ate in restaurants, but it always turned out that we just naturally separated—the blacks, the whites and the Latinos. One time after I was playing with the Mets, we stopped at a restaurant in Utica, New York. I was sitting with Nino Espinosa. After a while I noticed all the other players were eating and we had not even placed our orders. It really upset me and I called the server to our table.

"What's going on?" I said in a voice loud enough to be heard all over the restaurant. "Everybody's eating and you haven't even taken our order!"

About this time our manager, Yogi Berra, came over to our table. The server apologized, but the damage was already done. I was in no mood for apologies and I'd completely lost my appetite.

The color of my skin did not matter in Puerto Rico. People there celebrated my achievements. For example, soon after I went to the Braves, Yabucoa hosted a big event to honor their two hometown players in the big leagues—Jerry Morales, who played with the Padres at that time, and me. I was beginning to get used to playing before huge baseball crowds, but off the field I was still very shy.

On this occasion, Mercy and I were treated like celebrities, making me extremely uncomfortable. We were met at the San Juan airport, escorted to Yabucoa, seated in a convertible and paraded through the city. Mercy loved it. She smiled and waved at the crowds while I was dying of embarrassment from all the attention. It was a big celebration for our town with fireworks and live music—all broadcast on the local radio station. Ivy Ortiz, the guy who bought my first glove, was there too, directing the Sugar Kings Orchestra. He even wrote a song for me.

In time I began to accept the notoriety that comes with being a major league ballplayer. One thing I enjoyed about it was my fans, especially the kids. I'm a real softie when it comes to kids. I used to sign autographs for them until the last one had left the ballpark—leaving Mercy waiting in the car with our children. I hated seeing a player shove a kid aside and refuse an autograph. It broke my heart to see a happy little face dissolve onto the brink of tears, mouth turned down and shoulders slumped as he walked away. All I had to do was to sign my name or hit a few balls in a parking lot and I could send a youngster on his way with a big smile.

One time the Braves were in Philadelphia when I had a phone call inquiring about a kid who was pestering a front desk clerk at our hotel.

"There's a young guy down here named Ricky claiming he's your cousin," he said.

"Is it Ricky Pinto?" I asked.

"Do you know him?" The voice on the other end sounded surprised.

"Of course, I know him," I said. "He's my cousin. I'll be right down."

I turned to my roommate and said, "Come on, Aaron. I want you to meet someone."

Ricky lived with his mother in a low-income area of Philly, and whenever she saw me playing baseball on television, she would tell him, "That's your cousin."

"No, Mom, that's not my cousin," he'd say, not believing her. "That's Felix Millán."

Ricky decided to find out for himself if we were related. I'm glad he persisted until he found me in that Philadelphia hotel. We remain very close today and he never tires of telling people about our meeting in the hotel lobby, or another time when Hank and Tommie Aaron and I went to his neighborhood. All we had to do was show up, hit a few balls with the kids and we made the day for him and his friends. It always made me feel good to do something like that for the kids. That's the part of being a baseball personality that made me the happiest.

It was a very cold day and I had just signed with the Mets when this photo was taken January 31, 1973. Posing in the Mets' team cart at Shea Stadium with Manager Yogi Berra (center) are Ed Kranepool and Tug McGraw in the back. I'm in front with John Milner. (AP Photo)

8

Mets Life

I DON'T KNOW WHO WAS MOST EXCITED about my trade to the Mets, Mercy, Papi or the Puerto Ricans of New York. For Mercy it meant living near many of our Latino friends during baseball season. For Papi it meant plenty of people to talk with when he came to the States. And to Puerto Rican Mets fans it meant having one of their own to cheer for every day. I was ready for the move to New York.

Nobody, however, was prepared for the tragic events of New Year's Eve 1972 when Roberto Clemente died in an air crash off the coast of Puerto Rico. Roberto had an enormous heart. He was personally delivering relief supplies to victims of the December 23 earthquake in Managua, Nicaragua. He had invited a number of friends to go with him on that mission of mercy, including some of us Puerto Rican ballplayers. Most said no, not on New Year's Eve. That's a time when Puerto Rican families are together. Even if we are not together at any other time, we want to be surrounded by our families when a new year begins. It's tradition. We would not think of leaving home on that night.

Word of the tragedy spread across the island like a midsummer thunderstorm. Many were celebrating at New Year's Eve parties. I was asleep at home in Río Piedras when my good friend Rafael Aguayo awoke me with a phone call around two a.m.

"Clemente's gone," he said in a trembling voice.

"What do you mean?" I asked.

"The plane went down in the ocean. He's dead."

Baseball players in Puerto Rico are like a brotherhood. We may play on opposing teams, but we are friends. We may insult each other on a ball field, but we laugh together around a dinner table. We lost a brother when Clemente died. I remember his father hugging my neck at the funeral.

"Do you think they will find him, Felix?" he asked.

There was so much hope in his voice. I searched in vain for words of comfort. By that time I knew there was little chance of finding Roberto in the shark-infested waters off the coast of our island. My heart ached for his family.

"They'll do their best," I said. What more could I say?

New York baseball fans of Spanish Harlem may have been loyal to their Mets and Yankees, but if Puerto Ricans played on an opposing team, they cheered for the Puerto Ricans: Clemente and José Pagan of the Pirates, Sandy Alomar with the Angels, Cepeda and me with the Braves, and any of the other Puerto Ricans who played in the majors. We were Puertorriqueños and we always had a friendly place to go when we were in New York. Nonetheless, Mets fans were hungry for a Puerto Rican on their own team.

I did my best to make my people proud when the Braves played the Mets in New York, but I was never able to hit well against Seaver. Now I was on his team and I could not have been happier. Physically, I was at my prime in the spring of 1973 and I anticipated my best years in baseball lay just ahead of me. In the previous three seasons, the Mets had ended up in third place in the National League East, but I believed they still had a winning spirit.

They had a great bunch of players to work with. Five guys from 1969 were still there: Seaver, Jerry Grote, Jerry Koosman, Tug McGraw and Bud Harrelson. Rusty Staub and Willie Mays were also traded in when I went to the Mets. John Milner and Jon Matlack came up from the minors. Yogi Berra was our manager. From my first day in training camp, I felt like I'd been part of the team forever.

The Mets had lost about fifteen games in 1972 due to their inability to complete a double play. I knew Yogi expected me to help change that. With Harrelson at short stop we had the talent to do it.

Yogi had a way of bringing out the best in me. I never believed in giving a hundred and ten percent because it means taking dangerous risks that can result in mistakes. But ninety percent is not acceptable either. Ninety percent means not giving all I'm capable of giving. One hundred percent is my best. That is what I expected of myself, except perhaps for Yogi. Had it been possible, I would have given him one hundred and twenty percent.

In my first season in New York, I was the first player to score on opening day, coming in on Cleon Jones' home run. That seemed to set the stage for what would be a very good year for me. The Mets, however, got off to a dubious start.

Like every major league baseball player, I dreamed of winning a world title. I had high hopes of going to the World Series with the Mets. As the season progressed, it appeared that would not happen in 1973. By mid-August we were buried at the bottom of the league. Nothing short of another miracle like '69 would get us to the series. Fortunately, one teammate held out hope and inspired the rest of us to give it our best shot.

McGraw was the believer. He started prodding us with the famous phrase, "Ya Gotta Believe!" Before long he made believers of the rest of us, too. If we wanted it, we had to work for it and that's what we did. We won 24 of our last 33 games in the regular season. With only 82 wins, we barely squeaked into the top spot of the National League East.

Continuing to confound naysayers, we went on to beat the favored Cincinnati Reds for the National League pennant. Once again, the Mets had climbed from the bottom all the way to the top spot in the league. We were on our way to the World Series. Clearly, we were the underdogs going against the American League's Oakland Athletics. But underdogs or not, we had done what they said couldn't be done.

We traveled to California for the first two games of the series at the Oakland-Alameda County Coliseum. While neither team played well, the A's won the first game on October 13. Unfortunately, I made the most humiliating error of my career in that game when Bert Campaneris hit a grounder straight to me.

I do not know how many times I had picked up grounders like that. I would wait for the ball to bounce, pick it up and throw for the out. I had done it so many times I could do it in my sleep. However, Campaneris' grounder didn't bounce and that ball rolled right under my glove. Unbelievable! I let an easy roller go right past my feet. In a World Series, no less.

Mentally I was somewhere between disbelief, embarrassment, anger and humiliation. I remember looking into the stands where Mercy sat. I could see her dying of embarrassment for me. I just stood there and shrugged my shoulders in disbelief.

As the reality of my error began to sink in, I did not want to talk with anybody, especially reporters and certainly not my teammates. They tried their best to console me and get me back in the game. One after another they told me to forget it. Defensive coach Roy McMillan insisted it could happen to anybody.

Yeah, I thought. It can happen to anybody, but this does not happen to Felix Millán. I'm the guy my teammates depend on and I let them down.

Mays said he figured I would have rather died than face my teammates after missing that grounder, and he was right. Despite all their efforts to support me, I could not undo what I had done. The comment from my agent, Matt Mariola, did not help matters either.

"Now everybody knows you, Felix," he said, trying to make a joke of it.

That's not how I wanted to be known. A ballplayer wants to be remembered for his good plays and I had made plenty of them. The comment that meant the most to me came from Yogi when he said, "I wish every ball hit went to Felix."

While his confidence meant a lot, it did not erase the error from my record. Even today I occasionally see a film clip of that error on television. I always watch closely thinking maybe next time I'll catch it!

Of course, you don't have to watch or play many ball games to realize everybody makes mistakes. No matter what you do in life, chances are about 100 percent you will make them. As a young player, I prided myself in not making mistakes. I practiced and practiced and practiced to become a player my teammates could depend on to get the job done.

But nobody's perfect. Sooner or later we mess up. Missing that grounder taught me some powerful lessons, none more important than the uselessness of beating up myself over a mistake. The lesson I came away with is this: Give people a reason to trust you and they will forgive you even when you mess up. You have to forgive yourself, recognize your weaknesses, work on them and do better next time. That's what I had to do.

I swallowed my pride, reminded myself of what I could do and went back to work. I did much better in the second game, which went twelve innings and lasted more than four hours before we finally pulled ahead to take it 10-7. In that game I made one of the best defensive plays of the series when I ran into right field for a fly ball by Ray Fosse. Now there's a play I'd like to be remembered for.

When the series moved to Shea Stadium, the A's took game three while we took four and five. Returning to California, Oakland took the sixth game to tie the series, sending it into game seven. Although the A's took the last game and the title, in a series plagued by errors and poor hitting, the Mets had pulled off another season surprise. Not only did we go to the series, we took it all the way to seven games.

We did not win the only World Series in which I would play, but I'm grateful to have had the chance. That's the way it is in life. Sometimes the blessing is in just having a chance to play the game.

I played 153 games of the regular season in 1973, more than any other Met that year. With a .290 average I led the team in batting. I proved to be a solid consistent hitter with only 22 strikeouts in 638 times at bat, a Mets' season record I held until 2005. And I regained my 1971 National League standing as the toughest man to strike out.

I also set Mets' season records with 185 hits, 18 sacrifice hits, 82 runs, 155 singles and 4 triples. A .989 fielding average was my career high. I made only 9 errors, most of them throwing errors. With 16 hits and a .300 batting average in the week of June 17, I won the National League Player of the Week award. New York sports writers named me the Mets' Most Valuable Player of the Year.

After the World Series, I went back to Caguas for what turned into one of the best seasons ever for my Criollos.

First, we took the Puerto Rican League title for the first time since 1968. Then we went on to take the 1974 Caribbean World Series, which the Criollos had not done in twenty years. Baseball fans of Yabucoa were especially proud to have both of their hometown major league players—Morales and me—on the winning team for Puerto Rico. They had something else to be happy about, too.

At the end of the '73 season, the Padres traded Morales to the Cubs, which meant Yabucoa had hometown players in Chicago and New York, two cities with large Puerto Rican populations. When the Mets and Cubs played each other, Yabucoa fans often traveled to the games in New York or Chicago. They brought banners reading, "YABUCOA IS PROUD OF FELIX MILLÁN AND JERRY MORALES." It didn't matter which team won because either way, Yabucoa had a winner.

Those were great times for my hometown, and nobody enjoyed them more than Papi. Unfortunately, neither the Mets nor the Cubs would live up to their fans' expectations in 1974.

I was up in the air making this double play June 15, 1973. With San Diego Padres Gene Locklear out, I sent the ball to first for the second out. The following week I was named the National League player of the week. (AP Photo/Dave Pickoff)

9

Tough Times

WHILE WE METS BATTLED OUR WAY to the 1973 World Series, I continued to watch my friend Aaron hammering his way toward Babe Ruth's 714 home run record. The baseball world expected him to tie it in 1973, but he ended the season one homer shy. We would wait until the beginning of the 1974 season for the record-breaker.

I was in New York watching television when he tied the record on April 4 and again on April 8 when he whacked number 715 against the Los Angeles Dodgers in Atlanta. I remember seeing Braves relief pitcher Tom House reach up and catch the famous ball which went into the bullpen. Then he personally delivered it to Aaron. I wish I could have been there for that exciting moment in baseball history.

My 1974 season began with much less fanfare, of course, but it got off to a good start nonetheless when Ted Martinez graciously offered me his No. 17. I had worn No. 16 the previous season. Though I never expected to wear my old number again, it felt good to have it back. I would wear No. 17 all my remaining years with the Mets.

At 5-foot-10-inches tall and 172 pounds, I am relatively small compared to most major league baseball players, but I played a physical game. When I was with the Braves, I remember one time going hard into Johnny Bench, catcher for the Cincinnati Reds. It looked like I aimed to hit him out of the park. I did it another time with J.C. Martin who played with the Mets at that time. I had to play hard. Otherwise, I would get hurt.

Of course, in the heat of a game tempers can flare. Mine was no exception. I remember Don Sutton of the Dodgers hitting me with a pitch. I had hit a home run against him in our previous game. Pitchers never expected me to hit home runs. When I did, they felt insulted. Sutton wanted to get back at me and I did not appreciate it. I was ready to fight him right there on the field. Fortunately, we came to our senses instead of coming to blows. After that, whenever we met, Sutton would laugh—and whistle. All was forgiven.

Most confrontations between players are only verbal. One time, for example, Dave Campbell of the Braves threw me a slider. I made good contact and hit a clean line drive between first and second. I guess he thought he'd try to embarrass me.

"Hit the ball like a man!" he hollered.

"I hit 'em like you throw 'em," I responded with a smile.

A ballplayer remembers games for a lot of different reasons. A 1974 game I'll never forget went 25 innings, one of the longest games in major league history. We played the St.

Louis Cardinals at Shea Stadium on September 11. Each team scored a run in the first inning. The Mets moved ahead by two in the fifth, which the Cards matched in the top of the ninth, tying the game 3-3. Sixteen innings later, St. Louis scored to take the game. When it was all over, about three o'clock in the morning, I had been at bat 12 times.

I was the National League's toughest man to strike out again in 1974. In 518 times at bat, I fanned only 14 times, the Mets' season record to date. I also led the Mets with 121 singles and the National League with 24 sacrifice hits. Defensively, I finished the season with a .979 fielding average. Unfortunately, the Mets 71-90 win-loss record put us in the fifth spot of the National League East. Only the Cubs had a worse record than ours in the division. It was a bad year for Mets and Cubs fans everywhere and especially for those back home in Yabucoa.

My stats continued to grow in 1975. With only 28 strike-outs in my career record of 676 times at bat, I was the toughest man to strike out for the fourth time in five years. I also matched my Braves' achievement when I became the first in Mets' history to play 162 games of a regular season. I had the team's season high of 191 hits and played 1,456 innings, another all-time season high.

In my Mets career, I played nine games in which I had four or more hits. The most famous one involved a teammate from my Braves days, Joe Torre. After a trade to the Cardinals in 1969, he had come to the Mets in 1975. I batted ahead of him on July 21 in a game against Houston. I hit four singles, which Torre followed with four grounders to give the Astros four easy double plays. He set a National League record for hitting into four double plays in a single game and generously gave me credit for the "assists."

While these "assists" were never recorded in my official stats, Torre made the record books. Today, more than thirty years after that game, it continues to come up in interviews. When somebody asked me about it a few months ago, I suggested Torre could have avoided his famous record by simply hitting a home run.

The Mets managed to pull up to third place in the division in 1975. But it was not enough. By August of 1976 Coach Roy McMillan had replaced Yogi for the rest of the season. Although I had a good start in 1976 with a batting average of .346 at the end of April, it had dropped to .282 by the end of the season. I went to bat 531 times and struck out 19 times, earning second place in the National League for number of strikeouts per times at bat. My fielding percentage was a solid .977. For the fourth year in a row I led the Mets in singles.

Joe Frazier came on board in October to manage the Mets in 1977. He attempted to make a lot of changes that just did not work. For example, he wanted to change my stance and choke on the bat. When he said he could make a power hitter of me, I laughed.

"Look at this body," I said, pointing to my 172-pound frame. "You call this a power hitter?"

Other big changes were in store for the Mets in 1977, too. Seaver went to Cincinnati in a highly controversial trade that infuriated Mets fans. After all, Seaver was the face of the franchise. Why would a club trade its best pitcher? It didn't make sense to me. Frazier would soon be out, replaced by Torre. While several new names appeared on the Mets' roster, the team simply could not get its act together and we finished 1977 in last place. However, I did not play the final weeks of the season.

Little did I realize when I stepped into Three Rivers Stadium on August 12, it would be my last game with the Mets. Certainly it was not the way a ballplayer dreams of closing his major league baseball career.

We were up against the "fighting" Pittsburgh Pirates in the second game of a doubleheader with the score tied 3-3 in the sixth inning. The Pirates had men on first and second when the batter hit a slow grounder to shortstop Doug Flynn, who picked it up and threw it to me.

Our double play was going exactly as planned when all of a sudden the runner from first base slammed into me from behind like an NFL linebacker, sending me face down onto the ground. I came up spitting and shouting, and with the ball still in my fist I knocked him squarely in the face. I was prepared for the return punch by a guy who must have weighed twenty-five pounds more than I. However, instead of returning the punch as I expected, he picked me up by my legs and body slammed me to the ground. It turns out this guy, Ed Ott, had been a high school wrestler and football player. The benches emptied and my teammates carried me out on a stretcher. Ott was suspended while I went to surgery with a broken clavicle, dislocated shoulder and severely injured pride.

The Pirates went on to win the game in the twelfth inning, which put them in second place in the Eastern Division. That news barely made the next day's sports pages. Instead, the headlines were all about the fight. UPI sportswriter Fred McMane noted at that point in the season the Pirates were leading the league in fights and clearing the benches, suggesting they could possibly end up with the most players suspended in 1977, too.

Ott and I each apologized and the Pirates owner wrote me a very nice letter, also apologizing. Some thought I should sue but I would not do it. A lawsuit could not undo what had happened. After all, this was baseball, the game I loved. In my last season with the Mets, I played only 91 games, went to bat 314 times and struck out only 9 times. While I retained my .977 fielding average, my batting average slipped to .248.

One bright spot in 1977 was the creation of the Felix Millán Little League. Manny Rodriguez had a burden for the kids of New York City, especially the Latinos. He wanted to give them something to do in summer. What could be better than baseball? We were delighted when forty kids signed up for the first season. Today more than five hundred play in the league. Many of them are children of the original players.

While waiting for my shoulder to heal, another opportunity came that appealed to me. A former Braves teammate, Clete Boyer, who had played third base in Japan from 1972 to 1975, recommended me to the Yokohama Taiyo Whales, now the Yokohama BayStars in Japan's Central League.

Mercy and I discussed it. As with every big decision we made in our lives, we prayed about it, too. We had visited Japan when I played some exhibition games and we liked it very much. The more we considered it we thought we would enjoy living in Japan for a while. Certainly it would be a good experience for our children, too. I told the folks in Yokohama, "Show me the money," and the deal was done.

Even though I was excited about going to Japan, leaving New York and Shea Stadium was like leaving home. I have great memories from my days at Shea and a big part of my heart will always remain there. I shared those sentiments some time ago with TV host and Hall-of-Famer Ralph Kiner when I commented, "It's good to be home."

"I thought Puerto Rico was your home," he said.

"Shea Stadium will always be my home," I replied.

Time changes things, of course, and my old Shea Stadium is gone. It had been a good place for me. Good times, good people, good memories. I hope I gave the fans some good times, too.

When my major league career came to a close, I had been at bat 5,791 times in 1,480 games, striking out only 242 times. Defensively, I had played 12,666 innings, made 3,495 putouts, 3,846 assists and 855 double plays. I had a twelve-year fielding average of .980.

I would miss New York and the Mets by moving thousands of miles away to Japan. But I had no idea how much I would enjoy playing baseball there, or the blessings that lay ahead for me and my family. My Japan experience would confirm my faith that our God who knows the end from the beginning has a plan for every life. I believe that with all my heart.

10

Family Man

THANK GOD MERCY HAS BEEN BY MY SIDE all these
years. She is my helper, my counselor, my encourager, my
cheerleader and my best friend. From the day we were married, she helped put my dreams in order.

When I told her I had the opportunity to become a professional baseball player, she encouraged me to give it a
chance. When I couldn't find some young kid to practice
with, Mercy went to the park and pitched balls to me. When
I became discouraged and wanted to quit the minors, she
warned me of regrets.

"Give it another chance," she said.

I could always count on her cheering like crazy when I
made good plays, especially when I hit one of those rare
home runs. Even when I goofed up, she was there for me.

And all the while, she managed to take care of things at
home, too. She was in charge of moving every time I relo-
cated. She was in charge of our children's education and

getting them back and forth between the States and Puerto Rico. She was in charge of discipline when they needed it. When we bought the house for my parents, she was in charge of painting and choosing furniture. She also supervised construction of our house.

Mercy's father had given us a nice piece of land in Río Piedras after we got married. My Tío Andres agreed to build a house for us. At that time Mercy worked at a drugstore. It was the only job she ever had other than full-time mom and baseball player's wife, which I admit is not the easiest combination.

During the two years of construction, Mercy made sure the workers had all the supplies they needed. She even made breakfast and lunch for them. When our house was completed, we had a comfortable three-bedroom home with two porches and a separate trophy room for the baseball awards and photographs I was collecting. The house came out just the way we wanted. We lived there every winter for about twenty years. Today it's the home of a printing company.

Mercy and I wanted to begin our family soon after we married, but that did not seem to be in God's plan. Meanwhile, we became godparents to Mercedita. The little girl had begun spending so much time with us that her mother eventually asked us to take her full time. With Mercedita, we had a family, yet we yearned to give her brothers and sisters. After seven long years it finally happened.

We were the happiest couple on earth when we learned Mercy was pregnant with our first baby. She did everything she could to ensure we had a healthy child. She watched her diet. She followed her doctor's instructions. She read books and pamphlets. She even spent a lot of time reading the Bible. Mercy loved to read and I admired her for that.

I was playing winter ball in Puerto Rico when Bernie was born in December 1969 at the Presbyterian Hospital in Santurce. I had dreamed of having a son ever since I was a lonely soldier in Georgia. My dream had finally come true. From that day forward, my life was changed. I wanted only the best for Bernie. I wanted him to have a good life.

When I was on the road, I could hardly wait to get home to play with my son. I'd look at the little guy and see a future baseball player. At the same time I hoped in my heart he would never face some of the challenges I had, especially as a Latino. I wanted to be sure he learned English, but his first words were in Spanish, of course, because that is what we spoke at home. One time when he was about three years old, I found him jumping on our bed and I scolded him.

"¡No brinques mas en la cama o la vas a romper!" ("Stop jumping on the bed or you will break it!")

He gave me a sad look with his big brown eyes that just melted my heart and he responded in perfect English.

"Daddy, I didn't mean to do it."

I still get tears in my eyes when I think about that moment when I realized my kid could speak English—without a trace of Spanish accent. One of my most cherished dreams for him had come true. My son would never face the language barrier as I had.

Bernie had a fan from the day he was born. Mercy's good friend Gladys de la Cruz loved him. The two women were as close as sisters and spent a lot of time together when we were in Río Piedras. In fact, Gladys used to take Bernie to the Seventh-day Adventist church with her on Saturday mornings.

After a Friday night ball game, Mercy and I liked to sleep late the next day. However, about eight o'clock we were awakened by a loud knock-knock-knock at the front door. It was Gladys coming for Bernie. Mercy would go to the door in her nightgown, apologizing and explaining that our little boy was not yet dressed.

"Don't worry. I'll get him ready," Gladys would say. "You go back to bed."

She would get him up, give him a bath, dress and feed him and take him with her. We may not have appreciated being awakened at eight o'clock on Saturday morning, but we never worried when Bernie was with Gladys.

In 1972, three years after Bernie was born, God blessed us with our second child—the same year I received my second Gold Glove. Fortunately, I was playing winter ball in Puerto Rico again, which meant I was present for her birth, too—at the same hospital where Bernie was born. Mercy and I had agreed if the baby was a girl, we'd call her Femerlix, a combination of our names. However, when I told the nurse the name to put on the birth certificate she responded with a frown.

"That sounds like a boy's name," she said.

I didn't want my little girl to have a masculine name, so without even consulting Mercy, I changed the last letter from an "x" to an "e." I named her Femerlie. Mercy was not happy with me, but we had a healthy baby and that's what really mattered. Our daughter was a determined little girl who rarely smiled. I always saw my mother's personality in her and to this day when I look at Femerlie, I see Mami.

I cherished my time with our children. In fact, I taught them each to whistle. It became something of a family trademark and we had a lot of fun with it.

When time came for the children to go to school, I assumed they would go to public school, but Mercy wanted them to attend the Adventist academy near our home in Río Piedras because it had a good reputation for high standards. The kids liked the school and I was comfortable knowing they were getting a good education as well as Christian training.

During the regular baseball season, Mercedita, Bernie and Femerlie were in New York with us. Before school started each fall, they went back to Puerto Rico to stay with Tío Andres and Tía Oti until Mercy and I could join them after the post-season games.

Mercy had always been interested in health. One summer while we were in New York she took a vegetarian cooking class. I'll never forget the day she came home with two large shopping bags of canned foods I'd never heard of. She gave me that serious expression I'd seen only a few times in our married life.

"Felix, we need to talk," she announced.

I couldn't imagine what was on her mind. I did not think I had done anything wrong. Then she began telling me what she had learned in her cooking class, explaining why we should eat this and why we should not eat that.

I took a can from the shopping bag and read the label.

"What is this Vege-Burger?" I asked.

"I need it for some of the vegetarian recipes I got in the cooking class," she said.

I hesitated for a moment.

"Well, I guess we can try it," I said.

Frankly, I was doubtful. However, Mercy is a good cook. I figured I should at least let her try. That's the way I was with Mercy. She had good judgment and I'd learned it was usually best to listen to her. Although we didn't become vegetarians, the dishes she prepared were okay and we began to be even more conscious of eating a healthy diet than we already were.

Often when we were in Puerto Rico, Mercy attended church with Gladys and the children, and I went when I didn't have a ball game. We did not realize the influence the school and church were having on our children until one day when Mercedita took exception to some cranky comment my wife made to me.

"Why are you talking like that to my poor godfather?" she asked Mercy. "What's the matter with you?"

Mercy stopped abruptly while Mercedita kept right on lecturing her.

"You don't have Jesus in your heart. That's why you are acting like that," she said.

The little girl got my wife's attention. Mercy says Jesus used Mercedita to wake her up spiritually.

That was a turning point for my wife. She became much more serious about studying the Bible and attending church. After a while she decided to be baptized. I went to the service with her and witnessed for the first time a baptism by immersion. I figured if that's what Mercy wanted, I would not stand in her way although I made it clear that I personally had no interest in her new-found faith. Later, when the children also wanted to be baptized, I agreed to it—provided the decision was their own. As far as my faith was concerned, I had always believed I had Jesus in my heart and God was the Guide of my life. I did not need to be baptized to prove it.

We had big dreams for our children. As soon as Bernie was old enough, we got him into Little League Baseball. He was a good little player. Smart too. But like his father, he was happier playing ball than reading books. He once told me school made him feel like a lion in a cage, a feeling I understood completely. Mercedita and Femerlie, on the other hand, were good students.

Once again Mercy was in charge of moving us. All I did was pack a suitcase and catch a plane while she sorted, packed and took care of all the details of relocating to the other side of the world. Some wives would not have agreed to moving thousands of miles from friends and family, but Mercy did not hesitate. When I told her about my opportunity to play baseball in Japan, she said, "Let's give it a chance."

11

Blessed in Japan

I LEFT NEW YORK after the 1977 season ready to begin a new chapter in my baseball career. Traveling ahead of my family, I was in Yokohama when Mercy called from Honolulu, where she had stopped for a few days with Bernie and Femerlie. (Mercedita, a teen by this time, had chosen to stay in Puerto Rico with her friends and biological parents.) Mercy had tried to rent a car in Hawaii, only to discover we had no money in our bank account.

"It must be a mistake," I said. "There is more than $100,000 in that account."

"It is not there now" she insisted.

This was not how I had planned to begin my Japan experience. It seems my agent at that time had a gambling problem. We were not the only victims of his habit and he eventually went to jail. His wife feared I would sue her to try to get my money back. She begged me not to do it because she had children to support and no means of paying me. I knew it was not her fault. I hated losing the money, of course, but I always said I had nothing when I was born and whatever I made in baseball was a gain.

That was my last experience with an agent. Besides, I learned the Japanese were not keen on working with agents, preferring to deal with players one on one.

When I think about Japan I see narrow streets filled with people walking in every direction. It reminded me of the chickens I used to take care of in Puerto Rico—so many busy people going this way and that. I wondered where all of them could be going at the same time. I also remember seeing many cemeteries where family members cared for the gravesites of their ancestors.

Of course, Japan is well-known for its train system. Personally, I found it quite confusing. After boarding a train and riding for a half hour or so, I would reach another station that looked exactly like the previous one. I'd look around thinking, "I just came from here."

Another image that stays in my mind is large groups of children all dressed alike in school uniforms and hats. I never saw a place where so many people wear hats. The hat makers in Japan must be millionaires.

When it comes to baseball in Japan, I remember good friends, enthusiastic fans and the second grand slam of my career. I had looked forward to playing in Japan and I was not disappointed. In some ways it was tougher than American baseball. At the same time I found it less stressful.

Because the Japanese culture emphasizes group harmony, decisions in baseball are based on what is best for the entire team, not an individual. Players are expected to respect authority and avoid any behavior that might embarrass the team—both on and off the field. Obviously, it is a different culture from American baseball where players blow off steam, coaches and umpires get into hollering matches and agents negotiate lucrative contracts. All players in Japan are treated the same. Nobody gets special treatment. Exceptions are extremely rare.

Knowing that, I'm surprised my coaches gave me a choice when it came to pre-season training. I could either train with my Japanese teammates or train on my own. They said I knew my body and they respected that. Nonetheless, I chose to train with my teammates. I'd heard about their grueling routines but figured if I was playing with them, I needed to train with them, too. I never expected special treatment.

There were two things I did not like about spring training in Japan. First, it does not begin in spring. It begins in the dead of winter and Japan winters are freezing cold. In spite of the low temperatures, I reported early every morning for eight hours of strenuous training with my Japanese teammates. I remember sprinting up and down the steps of a Shinto shrine that must have had two hundred or three hundred steps. It was brutal. The second thing I did not like was raw salmon, a staple on the Japanese training menu. I never learned to eat it.

In Japan I had to do shadow swing drills, something I had never done in the United States. The idea is for a player to use his shadow and mirrors to measure head movement and develop muscle memory for a smooth and accurate swing. I did not put much value in those drills but the Japanese coaches did. They are strong on fundamentals. Even the most experienced player is expected to practice bunting, fielding and base running along with the younger less experienced ones.

I had arrived in Japan with the attitude that I came to play. I came to learn. As a foreigner I understood I was a guest. That meant adapting to the culture of my host country and I did my best to please. The biggest mistake some American players make in Japan (or any other country) is their inability or unwillingness to adapt to the local culture. When things do not go their way they lose their tempers and blow off. You just don't do that in Japan.

That is not to say Japanese baseball is without controversy. It's just that the Japanese have their own way of handling it without flaring tempers and heated arguments. Instead, the game is stopped when a problem or disagreement arises. The matter is discussed until a resolution is reached without loss of face by either side. These discussions can go on for an hour or so with a lot of bowing and apologizing. But this is how the Japanese resolve conflict in baseball, and in other areas of their lives, too.

I knew from the outset the Japanese played a different ball game even though the rules are the same. It is a different culture. American baseball is mostly physical while Japanese baseball is highly mental. American baseball values power. Japanese baseball is an art form. Americans take risks. The Japanese play it safe. It is all in the culture.

Japan has two baseball leagues, the Pacific and Central. At the end of the regular season the best team from each league competes for the national title in the Japan Series. Interestingly, most Japanese teams are known by the names of their corporate owners rather than their home cities. The Yokohama Taiyo Whales was an exception.

Owned by a fishing company as well as other corporations, the team has had various names throughout its history. With restrictions on whaling in the 1990s, "Whales" disappeared from their name and they are now known as the Yokohama BayStars.

I joined the Whales soon after they moved from Kawasaki to Yokohama where they had a large new American-style stadium. Typically, Japanese stadiums do not have parking lots. Because of this, they are built near train stations for the fans' convenience. As a consequence, games must end before the last train of the night departs. It does not matter whether the officials are discussing a controversial play or the score is tied, no game goes past 10:30 p.m. Also, no game lasts more than twelve innings. If the score is tied after twelve innings the winner is determined in the post-season. Cancelled games, rained-out games and tied games are resolved at the end of the season, which can go on for several weeks.

I played very well in Japan. In my three years with the Whales, I struck out only 52 times in 1,139 at bats. With a .346 hitting record in 1979, I was the first foreigner to win the leading hitter award in Japan. One of those hits was a grand slam.

Shigeru Kobayashi was the Tokyo Giants pitcher, one of Japan's best. With the bases loaded and knowing I was not a home run hitter, the young pitcher threw me a screwball, expecting an easy out on any base. I not only surprised Kobayashi and my teammates. I surprised myself, too, when I hit that ball deep into the bleachers.

I played my heart out in Japan. I loved the game and I was proud to be a part of the Whales team, which finished 1979 in second place, its best season ever. I also received the Japanese sportswriters' Best Nine Award in 1979—the only Whale to receive it that year. This annual award is given to the best nine players in the Central League and, with the addition of best designated hitter, best ten players in the Pacific League.

The Whales were very popular at that time and I loved the Japanese fans. They are loud, colorful and enthusiastic. In the States I was accustomed to organ music at the ballparks. In Japan they had big drums. Japanese baseball fans are extremely noisy, making for a very exciting atmosphere to play baseball. I loved it.

I found several practices in Japanese baseball to be different from what I was used to in the States. For example, a player received a Seiko watch when he hit a home run. I knew one guy from the Dodgers who had twenty-seven watches. He gave them away as Christmas presents. For an honor such as player of the month or for having a good year, a player might receive a big bag of rice. Unlike a monetary award, a bag of rice was not taxable.

Living in Japan was a wonderful experience for my family. Mercy, Bernie, Femerlie and I lived at the American Consulate. We shopped at the U.S. Army Post Exchange. Mercy found a church that provided English translation although she admits she could not understand a word of it. Bernie learned a little Japanese by spending a lot of time with me at the ballpark. Femerlie picked up some German from a playmate whose parents also lived at the Consulate. The Whales provided us a car and I eventually learned to drive on the "wrong" side of the road. While my sightseeing tours were limited mostly to baseball parks, Mercy and the children often traveled around the country on bicycles or by train.

When time came for school, Bernie and Femerlie returned to Puerto Rico to stay with Tío Andres and Tía Oti until Mercy and I could join them after all the post-season games.

Two individuals were very special to me in Japan. One was my manager Kaoru Betto, who I respectfully called Betto San. The other was my translator Yoichi Kokatzu. He accompanied me everywhere. I could not play baseball without Yoichi and we became very good friends. In fact, he even attended church with us and he always insisted that I offer thanks when we had meals together. He would not let me eat until I had prayed.

While I thoroughly enjoyed playing baseball in Japan, deep inside I began to wrestle with an issue that I knew could possibly end my playing days. It was a matter of my faith. I went to church with Mercy and the children when I could. In our home we observed the Sabbath from sunset Friday to sunset Saturday. I had been a Christian for a long time, but in Japan the Lord seemed to lay a burden on my heart that I simply could not shake.

The best I can explain is the Holy Spirit spoke to me through the example of my wife and children. The time had come for me to step up and join them as a Seventh-day Adventist Christian. I knew Mercy was praying for me to be baptized but I had never been convinced of the need for it. Baptism into the Adventist faith would mean no more Friday night or Saturday games for me. I struggled with the decision. I even prayed for God to take it away, but He didn't.

I needed a heart-to-heart talk with Betto San and the Whales manager Tadahiro Ushigome. These two men had always treated me fairly. I was not a young kid when I joined the Whales. From the beginning they had told me to do what I could and let them know when I'd had enough. However, what I needed to discuss with them had nothing to do with what my body could endure.

Once again Mercy and I found ourselves on our knees, asking God to lead us through this valley of an unknown future. Baseball was much more than just a game to me. It was my profession. Like a doctor or teacher or any other person who goes to school and takes a certain course of study in order to practice a profession, I had studied and trained to be a baseball player from the time I was a kid. Baseball was my passion. It's how I made a living and provided for my family. I had never had another job in my adult life.

I did my best to fit into the culture of Japanese baseball. I had not embarrassed the Whales in any way or brought undue attention to myself. I would not ask for a favor without good reason. Besides, I had a legal contract with the Whales. That agreement represented a commitment and I did not take it lightly.

All my life people had been able to trust me, to count on me. I had done well in Japan and I was well-liked. But now I wanted to change the rules in the middle of the game in a culture where everybody is treated the same, where nobody gets special treatment and exceptions are extremely rare.

At that time I did not know my friend Clete Boyer had created a big problem a few years earlier when he had asked the Whales for a day off every three games. His performance at third base had begun to slip and he thought giving his arm an extra day off would help. The Whales disagreed. Instead of getting an extra day off, Boyer got extra injections of vitamins. Had I known of his experience, I don't know whether I would have had the courage to ask for a day off for my religious beliefs. Boyer had asked for one day in three. I wanted only one in seven. The problem was I wanted the same day off every week. It was unheard of.

I don't remember exactly how I put it, but I tried as best I could to explain to Betto San and Ushigome that I had God in my heart and I needed to go to church with my family. All was going well until I asked for Friday nights and Saturdays off. They said that was impossible. I was an everyday player and they expected me to be available at any time like the other players.

However, in true Japanese style they agreed to discuss my request before giving me a final decision. I will never know what went on or what was said in their discussions because I was not there and I did not have an agent representing me. I left it all in God's hands.

A few days later Betto San and Ushigome had reached their decision and wanted to meet with me. I hoped they had decided to grant my request, but I also knew that if they did it would likely involve some kind of compromise in order to save face. Needless to say, I was anxious for their verdict.

After the customary Japanese greetings they began our meeting by acknowledging it was good for me to have a day of rest. I was glad they agreed with me on that point. With a prayer in my heart I listened as they continued, and when I heard their decision I could hardly contain my feelings. They had decided my name would no longer appear on the player roster for Friday night and Saturday games. In return I was expected to play every Saturday night and Sunday game.

That was exactly the arrangement I had hoped and prayed for. They never made a public acknowledgement or explanation for my regular absence from games, and I did nothing to draw attention to it either. We had reached an amicable agreement—albeit a highly unusual one—that all of us could live with. And it was accomplished without loss of face by anyone.

When my contract with the Whales expired, I thought probably the time had come to retire from playing baseball. After all, I wasn't getting any younger. The Nagoya team asked me to consider joining them, but I said no. It was time to go home.

Actually, I did not have definite plans for retirement. I figured I would take some college classes and find my niche in a new career, but I did not know what career that would be. Within a short time, however, I began to feel lonesome for baseball. I knew I still had a lot of the old game left in me. Like the catchy rhythm of an old Latin folksong that I could not get out of my head, baseball was always there. I could not imagine my life without it. When the Triple-A Red Devils of Mexico City came along with an offer, I was excited about another chance to play ball.

"Just one more year," I promised Mercy, "and then I'll retire."

12

Still in the Game

IN LIFE YOU HAVE GOOD EXPERIENCES and bad experiences. Mexico was a bad experience for me. It made me retire. Achieving a .316 batting average, I did well on the ball field, but that is where it stopped. After weeks of living in a second-class hotel room, I became disgusted with the whole situation. We had been promised an apartment, a car and a lot of other things that never materialized. I should have known. After all, I was not in the big leagues any more.

"It's time to quit," I told Mercy.

For once she did not tell me to give it another chance. Bernie and Femerlie were about twelve and ten years old at the time, and this was not the kind of life we wanted for them. In addition, I knew Bernie had the potential to be a fine baseball player and I needed to spend more time with him. Living in a lousy hotel room in Mexico City may have been no place to raise my kids, but it helped me put some personal things into perspective.

I had fulfilled my boyhood dream of a career in major league baseball at a time when such opportunities came to only a chosen few from my part of the world. I always tried to be a good ambassador for my people. After finishing my career in the major leagues, Japan had taken it into extra innings, and now it appeared that Mexico would be the final inning of my playing days. I had worked hard, enjoyed the glories of winning and suffered the agonies of defeat. I had a record to be proud of. As my career drew to a close, I could walk away without regrets, only gratitude for having had the chance to play.

Somewhere along the way I lost track of the exact number of games I played in addition to the 1,480 recorded in my major league stats. But adding them all together—minor leagues, major leagues, Japan, Mexico and seventeen winters in the Caribbean—I easily exceeded 2,000 games. While it is not a stat for any record book, it represents the achievement of a personal goal. I had enjoyed the best life I could have possibly imagined as a little boy growing up in Puerto Rico. Baseball was my passion and I was lucky enough to make it my career. Few people are blessed with that combination.

To be honest, something other than poor food, lousy housing and unfulfilled promises kept tugging at my heart. My managers and coaches in Mexico were not as accommodating to my religious beliefs as the Japanese had been. I wanted to be a baptized Seventh-day Adventist and publicly affirm my faith in Jesus Christ.

As soon as I finished the season with the Red Devils, we returned to Puerto Rico. It was great to be home. Over the next two or three years our lives revolved around our children and their activities, our families, our church and my education. I enrolled in the International Institute American World University, a school formerly in Hato Rey, where I earned a master's degree in marketing and management.

Time passed and I had not yet taken the step into the baptismal pool. In fact, I attended my Bible-study class for so long people started calling me the first elder of the visitors' class. It was just a matter of time, of course, until I would be baptized. I knew Mercy was praying for me to take my stand. However, this was a matter between God and me, and His timing is not the same for everyone.

You could say I looked at baptism in much the same way I regarded a baseball contract. It represented an agreement. It was a commitment. When I signed a contract, I committed to the terms of the agreement. Throughout my life, when I made a promise it meant something. The same goes for my marriage. When I married Mercy, I made a public commitment to her. I made promises. I gave her my word. And thanks to God, we have been together almost fifty years. Baptism meant making a public statement of my personal commitment to Christ. I had to do it without reservation.

It finally happened on a warm Friday evening in April 1982. Mercy and the children were there, of course, along with our church family. It actually turned into a much bigger event than any of us had planned. Every seat in the church, which holds about two hundred and fifty people, was full. More people lined up outside, crowding around the doorway and peering through the windows. Even people from the media came. I do not know how many baptisms make the local news, but mine did.

I was baptized by immersion, symbolizing a spiritual death to my old self and my commitment to a new life in Jesus. Taking that step at last gave me a wonderful sense of freedom and the peace that the Bible says passes all understanding. When I gave the Lord my word to follow Him, I promised by His grace to do what He required and I have never looked back. I'm glad Mercy never gave up on me and even more grateful that God did not give up on me either.

You never know what you might be asked to do when you make a commitment like that to the Lord. I certainly never dreamed I would be invited to teach a Bible class for eight- to ten-year-olds. I did not think I was cut out for the job, but I had this "contract" with the Lord. I had given Him my word. So I agreed to do it.

Teaching those youngsters turned out to be a very enjoyable experience—and another story to make local news. Noel Cruz, a reporter I had known ever since my baseball-playing days, came to the church to interview the kids, asking them how I measured up as a Bible teacher. Fortunately, they gave me a good grade.

I may have been retired but I still had baseball in my heart. I missed it and longed to get back in the game. Not as a player, of course. Those days were over. On a hunch, I phoned the Mets' home office. Something told me they might need a fielding coach. A few days later I was on my way to New York for an interview and shortly afterward hired as an infield instructor for the Mets rookie league in Port St. Lucie, Florida. I also worked as Latin American minor league coordinator for the Mets. I was back in the game again.

When Mercy and I returned to Florida in 1986, things had changed dramatically compared to when I joined the Kansas City minor league in Daytona Beach in 1964. I could live anywhere I chose in 1986, stay in any hotel and eat in any restaurant. The color of my skin and my language were no longer liabilities. In fact, my Spanish was an asset.

By this time baseball was attracting a lot of Latinos. As a bilingual instructor I could teach both American and Latino kids. I enjoyed this work and was able to help some young players who went on to the majors, such as Edgardo Alfonzo from Venezuela and Cuban-born shortstop Rey Ordonez. I also saw a lot of good players become discouraged and return to their homelands, due primarily to language, culture or homesickness. Even more kids would likely have gone home had there not been someone who spoke their language.

I remember, for example, a young Dominican player with the Mets, Quilvio Veras. He was ready to quit. His coaches had pegged him as a lazy kid who did not want to play anymore. When I had a chance to talk with him in Spanish, I discovered he had injured his shoulder. The Mets finally gave him time off to allow the shoulder to heal, but they eventually traded him to the Miami Marlins.

Although retirement finds me on the golf course more often these days than on the baseball field, I continue to be involved with the Mets and Major League Baseball. I have been a Major League Baseball instructor in Italy and Taiwan, working with talented kids who come from all over the world with dreams of making it to the big leagues. I have also worked as an instructor at the Roberto Clemente Sports City in San Juan.

I like working with kids. Of course, I'm especially proud of what the Felix Millán Little League does for kids in the East Village and Lower East Side of New York. It has been a godsend for keeping a lot of them off the streets and out of trouble.

A few years ago Bernie and I were involved in a baseball academy in Savannah, Georgia. I have also participated in some fantasy camps and I attend spring training games when I can. I cannot imagine a time when I will not be involved in baseball. Truthfully, I'd love to manage or coach, but Mercy is cautious. She says I take baseball too seriously. I say baseball is serious business. She is afraid it would not be good for my blood pressure. I say baseball is in my blood. I learned a long time ago it is usually best to listen to Mercy, but time will tell when I'm ready to hang it up.

I enjoy reuniting with other retired players, many of whom I played with or against in the major leagues. I had that opportunity in 1989 playing for the St. Lucie Legends of the Senior Professional Baseball Association. I did pretty well for an old-timer, hitting .269 in 31 games. Our manager was the late Bobby Bonds. We had played against each other when he was center fielder for San Francisco and he remembered me as a tough player. I laughed when I heard his comment to one of the other old-timers.

"I never saw a guy with more guts than Felix," he said.

Another time I was at a gathering of old-timers when a former player from the Caguas team handed me an envelope containing three hundred dollars.

"What's this?" I asked.

"I'm paying my debt," he said.

I had loaned him money many years earlier and had forgotten about it. He was one of the rare few to return borrowed money. In my day, baseball salaries were nothing like they are today. While I did not get a superstar's salary, I was paid okay for those times. It is a funny thing when a guy plays in a professional sport, some people look at him like a bank. The problem with loaning money is too often it means a double loss—loss of the money and loss of a friend, too. Twenty dollars loaned here, two hundred dollars there, and goodbye, friend. Even guys I played against and some I had never met before occasionally came to me for a "loan."

For instance, one time in Puerto Rico a man came to our house to explain that his daughter needed heart surgery. It was the first time I had met him. He wanted five thousand dollars. Mercy and I talked it over and finally decided to help. We never saw that man again.

It is not for me to judge him or the others we helped from time to time. I thank God that I had the money to give when they asked for it. I cannot forget that I came into the world with nothing, and I will go out with nothing. I might as well do some good with what God gives me.

13

The Winning Team

TWO OF THE MOST IMPORTANT PEOPLE in my life died in the 1990s—Papi in 1995 and Mami in 1997. Today they rest next to each other in an old cemetery overlooking the ball field where I dazzled local baseball fans as a teenager. A tall section of one rusty bleacher is all that remains as a reminder of a time when people of Yabucoa gathered to watch their favorite sons pitch fastballs and slap home runs.

Papi was ninety-six years old when he was hospitalized following a massive stroke. My brothers, sisters and I never left him alone from the day he entered the hospital until the day he died. His nurses said they had never seen a family show more love than we had for our Papi. On the day he died, it was my turn to stay with him. I mentioned that I should give him a shave.

"I need to cut that mustache," I said.

Papi smiled. Only moments later he quietly breathed his last breath.

Immediately a nurse came rushing into his room prepared to resuscitate him.

"Leave him alone," I said.

After all, he had lived a long life. He died knowing his children loved him. He had seen us all graduate from high school. Three had become baseball players and one had made it all the way to the big leagues. Victor Millán had realized a lifetime of dreams and was at peace. When we buried him, we placed his guiro in the casket with him. After that Cecilio, my only brother to take up the instrument, never had the heart to play again.

Not long after Papi died, Mami moved in with a lady in Yabucoa we called Doña Juanita. A devout Christian, she took very good care of my mother. They began each day having devotions together and she kept her radio tuned to a Christian station they both enjoyed. I was happy the day Mami told me she had accepted Jesus as her savior.

If my parents were to visit Yabucoa today, they would see a few changes as well as some things that have not changed at all. The old Central Roig shut down in 2000, the last of Puerto Rico's sugar mills to close. Our little house in El Cerro del Calvario is now in disrepair. The doors are boarded, the louvered shutters are rusted, and what is left of the corrugated roof is now overgrown with weeds. The house at La Pica, however, remains standing though hidden behind a wall of weeds as tall as sugarcane.

How I wish I could take Papi to the new stadium bearing my name where the Yabucoa Double-A team now plays. I can see him standing next to the bronze plaque bearing my image at the park entrance and bragging to people around him, "That's my son."

By the time Mercy and I went to Port St. Lucie, our children had grown. They were busy finishing school, getting jobs, marrying and establishing homes and families of their own. After college, Mercedita married Manuel Calero and she now works as an executive secretary in a law office. Bernie attended college for a short time, married and then divorced, and played six seasons in the Mets' minor leagues until a serious injury ended his dreams of a professional baseball career. Femerlie graduated from university and married Ruben Rivera, a schoolmate. Today she is a high school English teacher in Puerto Rico. (I hope no students fall asleep in her class.)

Mercy and I loved having children around our home. We were delighted when her seven-year-old niece Vilma spent a summer vacation with us in Port St. Lucie. The young girl was good company for Mercy while I worked, and apparently my wife showed her a good time. At the end of her visit she didn't want to go home. She asked if she could live with us permanently. Of course, that had to be her mother's decision. To shorten the story, her mother agreed to it and we welcomed Vilma into our hearts and home as one of our own. She lived with us until she went to college.

In Port St. Lucie, the Lord took me out of my comfort zone again. You could say I graduated from teaching to preaching. Mercy and I were attending an English-speaking church until Femerlie and Ruben came for a visit. During that time the four of us along with another couple from

Puerto Rico, met in our pastor's office for our Bible study in Spanish. We continued meeting there after Femerlie and Ruben left. Word quickly spread through the Spanish community and before long our group outgrew the pastor's office and moved to a larger room. In fact, we had enough people to hold church services. The problem was we needed a preacher.

Now, I had not bargained to do any preaching when I entered the baptismal pool several years earlier. But I had promised if asked to do something for the Lord, I would not deny Him. I did my best when my turn came to preach a sermon now and then, but to be honest, I will be happy not to do it again. The problem is a good preacher needs to do a lot of reading. I am just not cut out for that.

From our little group that began meeting in the pastor's office, two churches now serve the Spanish communities of Ft. Pierce and Port St. Lucie. Mercy and I make a personal effort to ensure there is a Spanish-speaking congregation wherever we happen to live.

We were in Puerto Rico in August 2008 when Mercy began complaining of not feeling well. She lacked energy and felt tired all the time. She blamed it on growing old, but I did not buy it. She was only in her mid-sixties, much too young and healthy to complain about growing old. I encouraged her to see her doctor. Surely he could give her some pills to make her feel better. After a lot of coaxing on my part she finally agreed to make an appointment with her physician.

Dr. Steven Rivas gave her a routine physical exam. Everything seemed to check out okay until he put her through a battery of stress tests. Clearly, everything was not okay because she flunked every one of them. I continued to believe he could give her a prescription and she would be feeling like new in no time. I was not prepared for what he said next. Mercy needed emergency heart surgery.

"It can't be," I told Dr. Rivas. The words would barely come out of my mouth as tears filled my eyes.

Dr. Rivas asked Mercy which cardiac surgeon she preferred. Of course, she had no reason to know the names of cardiovascular surgeons. Fortunately, she knew the right question to ask him.

"If your mother was having this surgery, which surgeon would you choose?"

"That would be Dr. José Rodriguez-Vega," he said.

"Then, he's my choice," Mercy replied.

I immediately phoned Femerlie and Mercedita who came as quickly as they could. I do not know what I would have done without them because I was a proverbial basket case. I know Mercy was nervous but she did not show her feelings like I did. I could not even speak a word without breaking into tears. Yes, the tough gutsy guy on the baseball field turned into a whimpering sap at the thought of what Mercy was about to endure.

After a while Dr. Rivas gave up trying to talk to me. He sent me out of the room while he explained the procedure to Femerlie and arranged for her mother to undergo a quadruple bypass surgery at the Cardiovascular Center of Puerto Rico and the Caribbean in San Juan. That six-and-one-half-hour procedure was the longest six and one-half hours of my life.

I was scared for Mercy, fearing the unknown and the possibility of the worst. I had relied on her all of our married life. She was always the one in charge. This time I had to leave God in charge of her. It was a real test of my faith. All I could do was pray and I prayed a lot. Finally, Dr. Rodriguez-Vega came into the room where we waited. I was relieved when he said the surgery had been successful.

While I could hardly wait to see Mercy, I was not fully prepared for what I saw. My beautiful wife lay expressionless in a hospital bed, asleep with a plastic mask over her mouth and hooked up to yards of tubing and strange-sounding machines with blinking lights.

Although the surgery had gone well, problems arose afterward. Mercy developed an infection and had to stay in the hospital an additional fifteen days. I could not imagine anything worse than a quadruple bypass, but she claims recovering from the infection was worse than the surgery. I thank God she came through the ordeal okay. I'm grateful that the problem was diagnosed before she suffered a life-threatening heart attack.

I have so many things to be grateful for in my life. From the time I was born to this day, God has blessed me abundantly. I cannot begin to name all the people who helped me or influenced my life in a positive way. Indeed, angels have accompanied me on this journey called life.

I am thankful I was born into the family of Victor and Anastasia Millán. At times my stomach may have been empty but my life was full and rich. They gave me a heritage that all the money in the world could not buy. I'm grateful to have grown up in Yabucoa where people took the dream of a shy little kid without shoes and made it their dream.

And I'm indebted to some of the most outstanding teachers in the history of baseball, men who identified the talent God gave me, helped make me the best second baseman I could be and never tried to make me something I wasn't. It was my privilege to play with some of the most notable players in the game, too. I did my best to win their confidence and they repaid me in more ways than I can count. We celebrated many victories together and stood by each other in times of defeat. They taught me there is no shame in making an error, only lessons to be learned.

Above all, I thank God for the love of Mercy. I think of what I would have missed had I not listened all the times she said, "Give it a chance." Without a doubt, the best advice she ever gave me was to give God a chance.

I like to say when I played with the Braves, I was on a winning team. The Mets was another winning team. But now I'm on the real winning team—the team of Jesus Christ. This is my testimony: When Jesus died on the cross, He died for me. When He rose from the grave, He won heaven for me. The thought humbles me and I am grateful—for His love, for His grace and for His wonderful mercy.

Yabucoa Valley today. While sugarcane is no longer produced here, the sugar mill with its identifying chimney (center) remains standing. This is where it all began for me: long walks to school, trying to hide my bare feet from my classmates, riding Don Paulino's horse to market, falling asleep in English class and, of course, baseball. Always baseball.

Felix Millán Selected Stats

Year	Games Played	Times At Bat	Strike Outs	Batting Average	Fielding Average
1966	37	91	6	.275	.973
1967	41	136	10	.235	.972
1968	149	570	26	.289	.980
1969	162	652	35	.267	.980
1970	142	590	23	.310	.979
1971	143	577	22	.289	.982
1972	125	498	28	.257	.987
1973	153	638	22	.290	.989
1974	136	518	14	.268	.979
1975	162	676	28	.283	.972
1976	139	531	19	.282	.977
1977	91	314	9	.248	.977
Totals	**1,480**	**5,791**	**242**	**.279**	**.980**

Source: Retrosheet.

References

PREFACE

Briskin, Shale (June 22, 2011). New York Mets: Top 10 Second Basemen in Team History. *Bleacher Report*. Retrieved November 7, 2011.

Hulka, James (August 5, 2008). All-Time Braves Lineup. *Bleacher Report*. Retrieved November 7, 2011.

Madio, Vinny (August 5, 2008). New York Mets All-Time Lineup. *Bleacher Report*. Retrieved February 8, 2012.

Stowe, Rich (June 1, 2011). MLB Power Rankings: Every Team's Greatest Second Baseman in History. *Bleacher Report*. Retrieved November 7, 2011.

CHAPTER 1

Puerto Rico Handbook (1946). Office of Information for Puerto Rico.

CHAPTER 2

Boyle, Robert H. 'el As' Is The Voice of America. *Sports Illustrated*, October 14, 1963. Retrieved February 18, 2012.

Madden, Bill. Canel's Voice Carries On. *New York Daily News*, September 18, 2005. Retrieved May 9, 2011.

_____. Buck Canel. *Viva Baseball*. Retrieved February 8, 2012.

CHAPTER 3

Complete lists of major league baseball players born in Puerto Rico are available on Baseball-Reference.com and Baseball Almanac.com.

CHAPTER 4

Ross, Ken. Hub Kittle. The Baseball Biography Project, Society of American Baseball Research. Retrieved November 7, 2010.

CHAPTER 5

A Roundup Of The Sports Information Of The Week. *Sports Illustrated*, October 16, 1967. Retrieved March 2, 2012.

Aaron, Hank, with Lonnie Wheeler, *I Had a Hammer: The Hank Aaron Story*. New York: HarperCollins Publishers. 1991.

Bryant, Howard, *The Last Hero: A Life of Henry Aaron*. New York: Pantheon Books. 2010.

Leonard, Laurence. Ambitious Millan-Cox Duo Braves' Box-Office Beauts. *Sporting News*, August 26, 1967.

CHAPTER 6

Lockwood, Wayne. Felix Millan Close to the Perfect Player, *Baseball Digest*, October 1969.

Ronberg, Gary. Felix Is One Sweet Ballplayer, *Sports Illustrated*, July 22, 1968. Retrieved March 5, 2012.

Tye, Larry. *Satchel, The Life and Times of an American Legend*. New York: Random House, 2009.

CHAPTER 8

Maraniss, David. *Clemente: The Passion and Grace of Baseball's Last Hero*. New York, Simon & Schuester Paperbacks, 2006.

CHAPTER 9

McMane, Fred. Ed Ott Tira Contra Terreno a Felix Millán, *El Mundo*, August 14, 1977.

CHAPTER 11

Albright, Jim. Japanese Yearly Best Nine Winners from 1940 to 2002. *The Baseball Guru*. Retrieved August 16, 2011.

Whiting, Robert. You've Gotta Have 'wa'. *SI Vault*, September 24, 1979. Retrieved June 8, 2011.

____. Shigeru Kobayashi, a great pitcher, died yesterday. Japan Press. Retrieved August 16, 2011.

Index